All About Tunisia

Grades 3-5

Written by Ruth Solski
Illustrated by Ric Ward and S&S Learning Materials

About the author: Ruth Solski was an educator for 30 years. Ruth has written many educational resources over the years and was the founder of S&S Learning Materials Limited. As a writer, her main goals are to provide teachers with a useful tool that they can implement in their classrooms to bring the joy of learning to children.

ISBN 978-1-55035-871-1
Copyright 2007
All Rights Reserved * Printed in Canada

Published in the United States by:
On The Mark Press
3909 Witmer Road PMB 175
Niagara Falls, New York 14305
www.onthemarkpress.com

Published in Canada by:
S&S Learning Materials
15 Dairy Avenue
Napanee, Ontario K7R 1M4
www.sslearning.com

At  Glance

Learning Expectations	An Introduction to Tunisia	Mapping Skills	Geographical Areas of Tunisia	Learning About Tunisia's Climate	Lifestyles in Tunisia	Tunisia's Economy	Tunisia's Culture	Tunisia's History
Mapping Skills								
• Locating a country using a map	•	•	•					
• Locating a country using a globe	•	•						
• Locating physical features		•	•					
• Locating rivers in Tunisia		•						
• Locating cities in Tunisia		•						
• Locating bodies of water		•						
• Locating bordering countries	•	•						
Literacy & Communication Skills								
• Reading to gather knowledge	•	•	•	•	•	•	•	•
• Making comparisons	•	•	•	•	•	•	•	•
• Recognizing symbols	•	•	•					
• Understanding terms	•	•	•					
• Recalling information			•	•	•	•	•	•
• Classifying information			•	•	•	•	•	•
• Brainstorming ideas			•	•	•	•	•	•
• Using context clues					•		•	
• Following directions	•	•	•	•	•	•	•	•
• Finding proof				•	•	•	•	•
• Locating information				•	•	•	•	•
• Researching a topic			•					•
• Developing oral skills	•	•	•	•	•	•	•	•
• Developing listening skills	•	•	•	•	•	•	•	•
• Developing writing skills						•	•	•

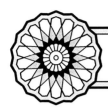

All About Tunisia

Table of Contents

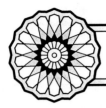

All About Tunisia

Teacher Assessment Rubric

Student's Name:_____

Criteria	Level 1	Level 2	Level 3	Level 4	Level
Understanding Concepts					
• Demonstrated the ability to locate places on a map and globe	Limited	Sometimes	Often	Frequently	
• Understood and used geographic terms	Limited	Sometimes	Often	Frequently	
• Demonstrated the ability to learn about a topic using reading skills	Limited	Sometimes	Often	Frequently	
Inquiry & Research Skills					
• Was able to apply a variety of research skills	Few	Sometimes	Most	All	
• Was able to gather information on a given topic	Limited	Sometimes	Good	Strong	
Relating Tunisia to One's Country					
• Demonstrated the ability to make comparisons on a variety of topics	Limited	Sometimes	Often	Frequently	
Communication Skills					
• Was able to use the terms and vocabulary pertaining to topic	Limited	Sometimes	Often	Frequently	
• Participated and added ideas to group discussions	Never	Seldom	Often	Frequently	
Inquiry & Research Skills					
• Was able to organize ideas in complete, sequential thoughts	Limited	Sometimes	Often	Frequently	
• Demonstrated creativity	Never	Sometimes	Often	Frequently	

Comments: _____

_____

_____

_____

_____

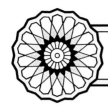

All About Tunisia

Student Self-Assessment Rubric

Name: _____

Put a check mark ✓ in the box that best describes your performance.

	Needs Improvement ★	Sometimes ★★	Almost Always ★★★	Always ★★★★
✓ I am a good listener.				
✓ I followed instructions and finished my work on time.				
✓ I completed all my work neatly and carefully.				
✓ I participated in all group discussions.				
✓ I listened well during lessons and while others were speaking.				
✓ I learned about Tunisia and its people and I can talk about what I learned.				
✓ I used all the resources available to answer questions.				
✓ I found it easy to read the information about Tunisia.				
✓ I know what I need to work on.				

1. I liked_____

2. I learned _____

3. I want to learn more about _____

All About Tunisia

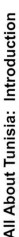

Vocabulary:

Each group of vocabulary words and phrases below could be printed on individual charts under the heading. These words could be discussed at the beginning of each lesson.

Tunisia's National Symbols: Tunisia's flag, Tunisia's Coat of Arms

Tunisia's Language: Arabic, French (business)

Tunisia's Money: Tunisian dinar

Tunisia's Physical Features: low mountains, Atlas Mountains, Tell Atlas Mountains, hills, grasslands, plain, coastline, Sahara Desert, plateau, oasis

Tunisia's Bodies of Water: Mediterranean Sea, Gulf of Hammamet, Gulf of Gabes, Gulf of Tunis, Mejerda River, salt lakes

Tunisia's Important Cities: Tunis (capital city), Sfax, Bizerte, Kairouan, Jerba

Tunisia's Climate: Mediterranean, hot dry summers, warm, wet winters, droughts

Tunisia's People: Arab, Berber, European, Jewish

Tunisian Clothing: fez (hat); jalabiyya (long, hooded cotton shirt with long or short sleeves); abaya (long-sleeved, slipover, one piece dress); hijab (consists of two pieces - one serves as a hair cap, the second is the head covering that you slip over the hair cap, worn by women); jilbab (long-sleeved type of jacket or coat that is worn over a light weight outfit); Kufi (man's Islamic hat); niqab (full face burqah or face veil that covers the entire face and eyes completely, only a slit to see through, worn by women); imama (a turban made of a long piece of material wrapped around the head of a man); isbal (trousers to the ankles); burnoos (a cloak with a hood); sifsari (a dress made of a long piece of material wrapped around a woman's body like an Indian sari); modern European dress

Tunisian Homes: gourbivilles (shanty towns outside cities); medina (old section of a city with narrow, winding streets); ville nouveau (new parts of a city); mud huts; tents; stone or concrete homes; adobe; white walls; blue doors; flat roofs; no front yards; very few windows; small; three storeys high; gourbi (tent) communities; underground homes; caves of Matmâta

Tunisian Wildlife: hyena, wild boar, jackal, gazelle, poisonous snakes (cobras, vipers), Barbary deer, antelope (addax, oryx), ostriches, maned mouflon, mongoose, porcupines, genets, foxes, suslik, desert varanid, scorpions, storks, hawks, eagles, wading birds, water birds

All About Tunisia

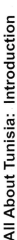

Tunisian Plants: cork, oak, pine, juniper, olive, pomegranate, almond, orange, date palm, grape vines, wild grasses, esparto grass, shrubs, citrus

Tunisian Foods: spicy, hot, couscous, meat, vegetables, semolina, lamb, beef, veal, seafood, shish kebabs, chakehouka (salad of tomatoes, onions, peppers, hard-boiled eggs), mechouia (grilled tomatoes, peppers, onions with olive oil, sliced hard-boiled eggs, lemon juice, and capers), chorba (soup), brik (small amounts of minced lamb, beef, or vegetables and an egg wrapped in a thin pastry and deep fried), bouza (rich, sticky sorghum and hazelnut cake), felfel mahchi (sweet peppers stuffed with meat, usually lamb, and served with a sauce), guenaoia (lamb or beef stew with chillies, okra, sweet peppers, and coriander), harissa (hot red pepper sauce used with any main dish), koucha (whole baby lamb baked in a clay case with rosemary), lalabi (rich garlicky soup made with chickpeas), makroud (semolina cake stuffed with dates, cinnamon, and grated orange peel); mhalbya (cake made with rice, nuts, and geranium water), salata batata (a hot potato salad flavored with caraway seeds), merquez (small, spicy sausages), tagine (a stew), j'bin (cheese), torshi (turnips marinated with lime juice and served with a sauce), yo-yo (doughnuts made with orange juice, deep fried then dipped in honey syrup)

Tunisian Sports: football, handball, rugby, golf

Tunisian Rural Life: gourbi (tent communities), herders, homes carved out of rock, underground homes, mud, stones, old lifestyle

Tunisian City Life: luxury homes, apartments, stone, adobe, concrete, white walls, blue doors, no front yards, few windows, small, two or three storeys high, flat rooftops, modern lifestyle

Tunisian Music: malouf (Tunisian music), lutes, guitars, violins, drums, sad

Tunisian Celebrations: birth of a child, marriage, death, January 1 - New Year's Day, January 10 - Eid al-Idha (Feast of the Sacrifice), January 31 - Hegira (Islamic New Year), March 20 - Independence Day, March 21 - Youth Day, April 9 - Martyr's Day, April 11 - Mouled (Prophet's Anniversary), May 1 - Labor Day, July 25 - Republic Day, August 13 - Women's Day, October 22 - 24 Eid al- Fitr (End of Ramadan)

Tunisian Arts and Crafts: wood, copper, textiles, leather, wrought iron, glass, ceramics, weave, blankets, rugs, carpets, grass mats, Berber rugs, jewelry

Tunisian Government: democratic republic, president, elected, prime minister, cabinet, governor, 13 provinces, independent

All About Tunisia

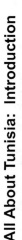

Teacher Input Suggestions

Planning Ahead:

Well in advance of completing this study of Tunisia in your classroom, begin collecting as many of the following items as possible:

- fiction or nonfiction books that pertain to Tunisia
- photographs and pictures of famous Tunisian people and places
- pictures of Tunisian people and the flag
- pictures of Tunisia's animals, birds, and plants
- maps of Tunisia, Africa, and the World
- a globe
- recordings of Tunisian music
- samples of Tunisian traditional dress
- samples of Tunisian crafts
- videos and DVDs of Tunisia

Place a variety of the articles collected at an interest center on Tunisia to stimulate student interest and curiosity in the country.

Use pictures to create a bulletin board display entitled "All About Tunisia".

Teacher-Directed Lessons and Student Activities

This book contains 8 Teacher-Directed Activity Lessons that have teacher support information on Tunisia and ideas on how to implement it into the classroom. There are 33 reproducible Student Activities that correspond with the various lessons. They may be done independently or as a large group reading activity with follow-up assignments.

The information pages and activity pages could be collated to form a booklet on Tunisia. The cover of the booklet could be made out of construction paper. On the cover the students could illustrate a picture pertaining to Tunisia and label it "All About Tunisia".

or

The information pages and activity pages could be completed and colored and then glued into the students' notebooks with an illustrated and labeled title page at the beginning called "All About Tunisia".

An Introduction to Tunisia

A. Reproduce "Student Activity 1: Learning About Tunisia" for your students.

B. Read the information to your class or with your class depending on their reading ability.

C. Have your students locate the answers to the following questions in the information.

1. Where is Tunisia located in our world? (**Continent of Africa**) Have your students locate the Continent of Africa and Tunisia on a world map and globe.

2. How big is Tunisia? (**twice the size of New Brunswick or twice the size of the state of South Carolina**)

3. Describe the Tunisian flag. (**red and white; white disc with red crescent and star on a red background**)

4. What does the disc stand for on Tunisia's flag? (**the sun**)

5. What do the red crescent and red star represent? (**symbols of Islam**)

6. What is Islam? (**Muslim religion**)

7. What are the three symbols on Tunisia's coat of arms? (**ship, lion, set of scales**)

8. What does each symbol on the coat of arms represent? (**ship - freedom; lion - order; scales - balance of justice**)

9. What is Tunisia's national food? (**couscous**)

10. Has anyone in the class ever eaten or tasted couscous? (**Answers may vary.**) What food do we use with meat dishes that is similar to couscous? (**rice**)

11. What is Tunisia's national sport? (**soccer**)

12. How many people live in Tunisia? (**around 10 million people**)

13. Where do the people mainly live in Tunisia? (**in or around cities**)

14. What language is mainly spoken in Tunisia? (**Arabic**)

15. What is the capital city of Tunisia? (**Tunis**)

D. Reproduce "Student Activity 2: Tunisia's Sights and Symbols" for your students. Discuss the various pictures and relay the following information. The students are to color the pictures that pertain to Tunisia.

Tunisian Flag: The Tunisian flag is a national symbol of Tunisia. It has a bright red background. On the background is a white disc or circle that represents the sun. On the inside of the disc is a red crescent and a red, five-pointed star. The red color represents Tunisia's resistance against outside forces. The red crescent and red star are symbols of Islam. The crescent is the same shape of the waxing moon and brings good luck.

Tunisia's Coat of Arms: Tunisia's Coat of Arms is a shield that bears the motto "order, freedom, and justice". On the shield are three images. The images are of a lion, a ship, and a set of balance scales. The lion represents order, the ship freedom, and the balance scales justice.

An Introduction to Tunisia

Dates: The date is an oblong fruit that measures 2.5 to 5 centimeters (1 to 2 inches) in length. The date has a thick, sweet flesh covered by a tough skin that surrounds a single large seed. Dates vary in color. Some are yellow to orange, red, or green depending on the kind. Dates grow in clusters at the end of stalks. A single cluster may contain 600 to 1,700 dates. Dates grow on date palm trees.

Couscous: Couscous is a staple food of the Maghreb region of Africa. It was first made and eaten by the Berbers who have lived in Tunisia for hundreds of years. Couscous consists of small granules which are made by rolling and shaping moistened semolina wheat and then coating them with finely ground wheat flour. The grains are about 1 mm (1/26 inch) in diameter after cooking. It is prepared by steaming and is served under a meat or vegetable stew. It can be eaten alone, flavored or plain, warm or cold, as a dessert, or as a side dish.

Date Palm Tree: Date palm trees grow in hot, dry climates and especially on desert oases where few plants grow. The date palm is one of the oldest crop plants. People began cultivating date palms at least 5,000 years ago. Date palms grow as tall as 30 meters (100 feet). They have straight, rough trunks. Feather-like leaves from 3 to 6 meters (10 to 20 feet) long fan out from the top of the trunk. Flowers bloom on the trees between February and June. The fruit ripens from June to December. Date palms are used for food, shade, building materials, and fuel.

Oasis: An oasis is a fertile area in a desert where underground water comes close enough to the surface for springs and wells to exist. Some oases are small and can only support a few people while others are large enough to support millions of people. Large oases contain farms and towns. Date palms and other plants are able to grow in an oasis.

Minaret: A minaret is a tall, slender tower attached to a mosque. From the top of a minaret a "muezzin" (crier) calls the Muslims to prayer five times each day. Each minaret has more than one balcony where the muezzin can stand. The minaret can be round, square, or many-sided. Most are made of brick or stone and contain an inside staircase.

Mosque: A mosque is a building used by Muslims for worship. They are also used for religious instruction, as tombs, and as temporary homes for traveling scholars. A typical mosque has a courtyard surrounded by four halls called "iwans". In the courtyard is a fountain or well for ceremonial washing. Walls and floors are decorated with painted or tile patterns or with religious quotations in elegant handwriting called calligraphy. Most mosques have one to six towers called minarets from which muezzins (criers) call the Muslims to prayer. Many mosques have a pulpit called a "mimbar".

Camel: A camel is a large, strong animal that can travel great distances across hot, dry deserts with little food or water. Camels serve the people of desert communities in many ways. In lands at the edge of deserts, camels pull plows, turn water wheels to irrigate fields, and carry grain to market. Deep in the desert, camels are the main source of food, clothing, and shelter. Young camels are eaten, butter is made from the fat in the camel's hump, and its milk is made into cheese or used for drinking. The camel's coat supplies wool and leather for clothing, blankets, and tents.

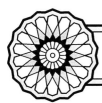

Learning About Tunisia

Marbaha! My name is Mona. I live in a large city called Tunis in the country of Tunisia.

Welcome to my country!

Look for Tunisia on a world map.

Tunisia is found in the continent of Africa. It lies in Northern Africa and is bordered on the north by the Mediterranean Sea, on the west by Algeria, and on the southeast by Libya. It is one of the smallest countries in Africa and is twice the size of the province of New Brunswick and the State of South Carolina in the United States.

countries in North Africa. The other Arab countries are Egypt, Libya, Algeria, and Morocco. Outsiders from other countries wanted our rich farmland and our safe ports. Tunisia has been ruled by the Phoenicians, the Romans, the Turks, the Arabs, and finally the French. In 1956, after many years of discussion with France, Tunisia won its independence.

Sidi Bou Said, on the Mediterranean coast

Romans built this amphitheater when they ruled Tunisia

My country has a very long history and people have lived in it for centuries. Tunisia is one of the Arab

Tunisia's flag is one of our national symbols. It is bright red with a white disc or circle. Inside the disc is a red crescent and a red star. The red color

Learning About Tunisia

is a symbol of our resistance against outside forces. The disc in the middle stands for the sun. The red crescent and star are symbols of Islam and are considered lucky ones. Our coat of arms is another national symbol. It is in the shape of a shield. On the shield is a ship, a lion, and a set of scales. The ship stands for freedom, the lion for order, and the scales for the balance of justice.

Tunisia's national dish is called couscous. Couscous is made up of round bead-like pieces of rolled, wet semolina wheat that are coated with finely-ground wheat flour. It is often served with different meat dishes. Our national sport is soccer or football. It is played on large soccer fields and on the streets in many towns and cities.

The population of Tunisia is around ten million people. Most of the people live in or close to cities. Others live on farms and in rural communities. The main language spoken is Arabic and French is used for doing business.

Our capital city is Tunis. It is found near the Gulf of Tunis. It sits on the shores of a lake that joins it to the Mediterranean Sea.

You will find my country very different and very interesting!

A mosque tower in Tunis

The market after closing time in downtown Tunis

Tunisia's Sights and Symbols

In Tunisia, everyone loves to eat couscous at their meals. There are many other things that belong to our country.

Color the following sights and symbols of Tunisia neatly.

Tunisia's Flag	**Tunisia's Coat-of-Arms**	**Dates**

Couscous	**Date Palm Tree**	**Oasis**

Minaret	**Mosque**	**Camel**

Mapping Skills

A. Reproduce the map in "Africa on Student Activity 3: Where Is Tunisia?" and give them out to your students.

B. Using a world map have a student locate Africa and Tunisia. Have your students locate Tunisia on their maps. It is number 1 on the map of Africa. Its name should be printed on line 1. Instruct the students to color Tunisia red.

C. Have the students locate the following countries that border Tunisia and the body of water and record their names on the lines provided.

   1. What is the name of the country that borders Tunisia to the west? **(Algeria - Line 2)**

   2. What is the name of the country that borders Tunisia to the east? **(Libya - Line 3)**

   3. What is the name of the country east of Libya? **(Egypt - Line 4)**

   4. What is the name of the country west of Algeria? **(Morocco - Line 5)**

   5. What is the name of the large body of water off Tunisia's coast? **(Mediterranean Sea - Line 6)**

   6. Explain to your students that the area in which the countries of Morocco, Algeria, Tunisia, and Libya are found in northwest Africa is called the "Maghreb". In this area the people live with two competing cultures; the culture of the West, which they have experienced through colonialism and have defined as modern; and their Arabic heritage, which for hundreds of years produced great cultural achievements which were looked down upon during colonial times. Tunisians have a strong sense of ethnic identity and cultural pride but also have a more modern outlook and are able to balance their traditional Arab heritage with new modern ways.

   7. Why do you think the Mediterranean Sea is very important to Tunisia? **(Answers may vary.)**

D. Reproduce "Student Activity 4: Labeling a Map of Tunisia" for your students. Discuss the numbered places on the map of Tunisia. As you proceed through the map, have the students record the name of the city, river, and bodies of water on the lines provided. Discuss the importance of each one using the following information.

Tunis: Tunis is the country's capital city and the largest one in Tunisia. It is an ancient city and was a very important religious center. Tunis has one of the oldest mosques called the Ez-Zitouna Mosque which is now a part of the University of Tunis. It is built in the center of Tunis or the "medina". The "souks" or markets and old city buildings are built around it.

Mapping Skills

Tunis' streets are narrow and winding and are filled with monuments and historical buildings. This part of Tunis has been designated as a world heritage site by the United Nation's Educational, Scientific, and Cultural Organization called UNESCO.

Bizerte: Bizerte is the northernmost city in all of Africa. It is the fifth largest city in Tunisia. Bizerte is located on the coast and is an important port. Between Bizerte and the border of Algeria is rich farmland. At one time it supplied the Roman Empire with grain. The ruins of many Roman towns and villages are seen in this region.

Bizerte was once an important Phoenician trading post. Its narrow streets lead to the old port. The medina or city center is filled with beautiful mosques, souks (markets), and Moorish houses. The new part of the city built by the French has wide streets, modern buildings, and gardens.

Sousse: Sousse is Tunisia's fourth largest city. It is located on the coast in central Tunis. Its wide beaches and warm climate attract many tourists. It has a medina that has an old mosque that was once used to defend the port from invaders. The walls of the courtyard contain small rooms where soldiers lived. Many museums and tourist attractions are found in the medina as well. The modern area of Sousse was built by the French and has beautiful homes, hotels, and other buildings on wide streets.

Kairouan: Kairouan is one of the most historic and oldest cities in Tunisia that is not located on the coast. It was the first Islamic city built in the Maghreb by conquering Arabs over 13 centuries ago. Arab warriors spread the teaching of Islam and Arabic culture among the Berber people living in the area. Kairouan is an important spiritual center for Muslims and has steadily grown in size and is the sixth largest city in Tunisia. It is an important manufacturing center and is famous for its traditional crafts, rugs, copperware, and pointed shoes.

Sfax: Sfax is also called Sahel. It is the second largest city in Tunisia. Sfax is located on the coast of central Tunisia. It is a large industrial city with an important port for business and fishing. It is a major seaport that handles the export of olive oil and phosphates. Sfax has two distinct districts as well. The medina was built up over the old port and many of its people still shop at the souks or markets.

Jerba: Jerba is not a city but an island and is found off the North African coast. There are no major cities on Jerba but there are several large towns. Jerba is home to a unique community in Tunisia. Many of the islanders are Berber rather than Arab and speak their own original language of Jerba, which is a Berber dialect, as well as Arabic. Most of the people live in

Mapping Skills

whitewashed homes with cone-shaped roofs. The main industry on Jerba is tourism. Water supply is limited on the island and has restricted farming. At one time the people made handicrafts and fished for a living.

Mediterranean Sea: The Mediterranean Sea is almost completely surrounded by land. Europe lies to the north, Asia to the east, and Africa to the south. It is connected to the Atlantic Ocean by the Strait of Gibraltar. Several other seas are connected to the Mediterranean Sea such as the Adriatic Sea, Ionian Sea, Ligurian Sea, Tyrrhenian Sea, and the Black Sea. It is connected to the Red Sea by the Suez Canal.

The water in the Mediterranean Sea is saltier than the water in the Atlantic Ocean as it evaporates faster due to the warm, dry climate. The Mediterranean Sea is an important source of food for the people in the area. It is also a very important waterway that links Europe, the Middle East, and Asia. The Mediterranean region attracts millions of tourists yearly.

Gulf of Tunis: The Gulf of Tunis is a large gulf off the coast of northeastern Tunisia. The capital city of Tunis lies at the southern edge of the gulf. It has beautiful beaches.

Gulf of Hammamet: The Gulf of Hammamet is a large gulf in northeastern Tunisia. This gulf shelters miles of sandy beaches and sparkling seas.

Gulf of Gabes: The Gulf of Gabes is located on the east coast of Tunisia in northern Africa. It is 100 km (60 miles) long and 100 km (60 miles) wide. It is bounded by the Kerkena Islands on the northeast and by Jerba Island on the southeast. During the spring it has very high tides.

Mejerdah River: The Mejerdah River is found in Tunisia and Algeria. It is 45 km long (28 miles) and is the longest river in Tunisia. It begins in the mountains in Algeria and flows through Tunisia to the Gulf of Tunis. It is the only river that does not dry up during the hot season. The Mejerdah river provides water for the people to use and is dammed in several places to provide water for irrigation for farms that grow wheat. This river has been fought over by numerous early invaders.

Where Is Tunisia?

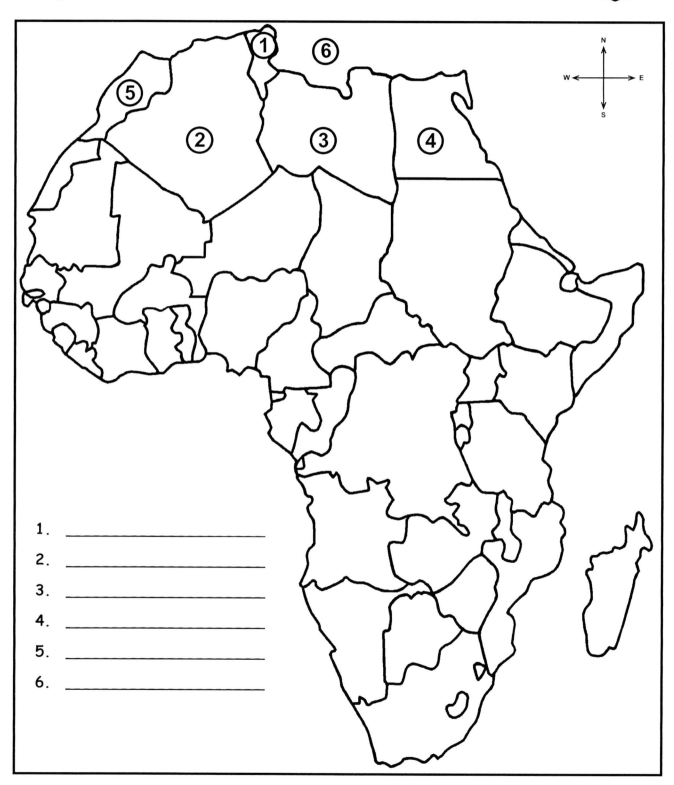

1. _____

2. _____

3. _____

4. _____

5. _____

6. _____

Labeling a Map of Tunisia

1. _____

2. _____

3. _____

4. _____

5. _____

6. _____

7. _____

8. _____

9. _____

10. _____

11. _____

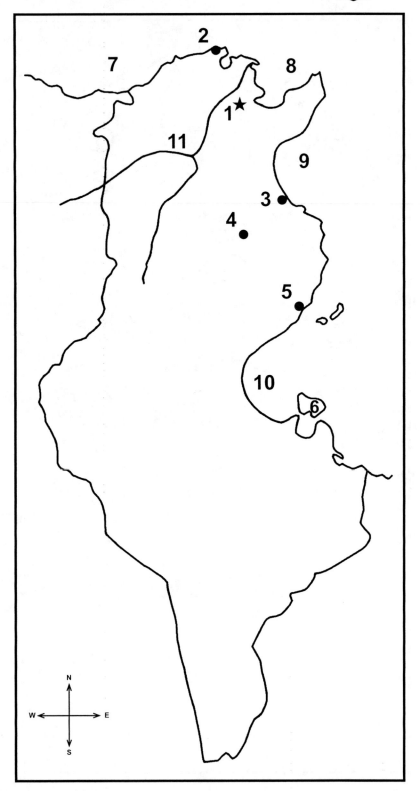

Geographical Areas of Tunisia

A. Discuss the following geographical terms and their meanings with your students.

plain: a region of horizontal, level rock layers or gently rolling land of low elevation; a flat stretch of land or prairie

plateau: a large, level area higher than the surrounding land made of horizontal layers of rock; a large, high plain

steppe: a treeless plain similar to a prairie; its grasses are short not long; it can be semi-desert or covered with grass or shrubs

island: a piece of land completely surrounded by water

coast: the land bordering the sea, the seashore

gulf: a wide, very large bay; an arm of an ocean or a sea extending into the land

lagoon: a shallow body of water separated from the sea by a narrow strip of land

desert: a dry land with little rainfall where few or no plants can grow

oasis: a fertile area in the desert with enough water for permanent plant growth

Compare these landforms to the landforms in your country. Which ones are similar? (**plain, steppe, plateau, coast, gulf**) Which ones are different? (**lagoon, desert, oasis**)

B. Reproduce "Student Activity 5: Tunisia the Land" for your students.

C. Explain to your students that the landforms previously discussed are also found in Tunisia. Have your students read the information on Tunisia's geographical areas as a group or as an independent reading activity. As the reading progresses try to point out the various physical features on a map that shows Tunisia's physical features.

D. Using the information have your students locate the answers to the following questions.

1. What two groups of mountains are found in northern Tunisia? (**Tell Atlas and Atlas Mountains**)

2. What is the name of the main river in Tunisia? (**Mejerda River**)

3. Where is the Mejerda River located in Tunisia? (**in a valley between the Tell Atlas and Atlas Mountains**)

4. How is the Mejerda River Valley used? (**for farming**)

5. What crops are grown in the Mejerda River Valley? **(grains)**

6. What is Tunisia's coastline like from the Gulf of Tunis to the Gulf of Gabes? **(has excellent harbors and sandy beaches)**

7. What landform is found inland in this area? **(coastal plains)**

8. Why are these plains important to Tunisia? **(have fertile soil; citrus fruits and vegetables are grown)**

9. Name fruits that belong to the citrus family. **(oranges, lemons, grapefruits, tangerines, limes, tangelos, mandarin oranges)**

10. Where is the Sahel area located in Tunisia? **(on a coastal plain between the Gulf of Hammamet and the Gulf of Gabes)**

11. Why is the Sahel such an important area in Tunisia? **(nearly half the people in Tunisia live in this area)**

12. What is the name of the area tourists love to visit? **(Kerkennah Islands)**

13. What landform is found in central Tunisia? **(a wide, flat plateau)**

14. Why is this area not used for farming and has few towns and cities? **(dry, hot, little rainfall; few plants grow)**

15. Why have nomadic herders stopped using this plateau to feed their animals? **(the Sahara desert is slowly moving northward)**

16. What landform is found in the southern-most part of Tunisia? **(Sahara Desert)**

17. What are the fertile areas in the Sahara Desert called? **(oases)**

18. What plant grows well in an oasis? **(date palm tree)**

19. How does an oasis remain in the desert? **(has water that comes from under the ground)**

E. Reproduce the "Student Activity 6: Tunisia the Land" worksheet for your students. The students are to put a check mark in the box beside each true statement and an X beside each false statement.

The following boxes may have a check mark or an X.

 **Answer Key:**

1. X	2. X	3. ✓	4. X	5. ✓
6. X	7. ✓	8. ✓	9. X	10. ✓
11. X	12. ✓			

Tunisia the Land

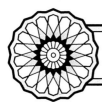

My country belongs to three different regions. They are Africa, the Maghreb, and the Mediterranean. The Maghreb is an Arabic word that means "the land of the setting sun". This region includes the countries of Morocco, Algeria, Tunisia, and sometimes Libya.

The Atlas Mountains

Tunisia is made up of four different areas. In northern Tunisia are two groups of mountains. They are called the Tell Atlas and the Atlas Mountains. The Tell Atlas Mountains are lower than the Atlas Mountains. The mountains often receive 102 centimeters (40 inches) of rain each year and snow can be seen on their peaks. Between the Tell Atlas and the Atlas Mountains flows the Mejerda River from Algeria to the Gulf of Tunis. It is the only major river in Tunisia with a wide, fertile valley used for farming. Grain is grown in the valley and animals are raised.

Along Tunisia's Mediterranean coastline from the Gulf of Tunis to the Gulf of Gabes are excellent harbors and sandy beaches. Inland from the Mediterranean Sea are coastal plains. These plains have fertile soil, and citrus fruits and vegetables are grown there.

Hammamet Beach

Between the Gulf of Hammamet and the Gulf of Gabes, the coastline has wide beaches and good harbors.

Tunisia the Land

Inland from the coast in the central part of Tunisia is a humid coastal plain and low hills. This area of Tunisia is called the Sahel. This is a very important region and is home to nearly half of the people in Tunisia. This area is very old and goes back to the days of the Roman Empire. The Sahel contains ancient villages and olive, pomegranate, and almond orchards.

Off the coast from the city of Sfax are the Kerkennah Islands. These islands are covered with palm trees and vineyards surrounded by quiet lagoons. It is a tourist paradise.

In central Tunisia lies a wide, flat plateau. It is divided into sections called the High Steppe and the Low Steppe. This plateau is dry and hot and receives little rain. Only a few plants and scrub bushes can grow. At one time nomadic herders used the grass that grew on the plateau to feed their animals. Today there is no grass as the Sahara desert has slowly moved northward. There are very few towns or cities in this area.

South of the central plateau Tunisia is very barren. Its climate is hotter and drier. During the winter, rain falls and fills low areas creating shallow, salt water lakes which dry up during the summer months. Further south the land becomes part of the Sahara Desert.

The Sahara Desert

Some areas of the desert do not receive any rain for years. Nothing grows in the desert except in oases, which are fertile areas that get water from underground springs. The people who live in an oasis community depend a great deal on their date palm trees.

A Tunisian palm oasis

Tunisia the Land

The areas in my country are quite different from most countries. How well did you read and how much do you remember about areas in Tunisia?

Put an X in the box if the sentence is false or a ✓ in the box if the sentence is true.

1. ☐ There are no mountains in Tunisia.

2. ☐ Many rivers flow through Tunisia to the Mediterranean Sea.

3. ☐ Citrus fruits and grains grow on a fertile inland plain between the Gulf of Tunis and the Gulf of Gabes.

4. ☐ The Sahara Desert is filled with many oases that grow date palm trees.

5. ☐ Islands near the city of Sfax are popular with tourists.

6. ☐ The Sahara Desert is found in northern Tunisia near some mountains.

7. ☐ The Sahel is an area in Tunisia where most of the people live and work.

8. ☐ The weather in the Sahara Desert is hotter and drier than in any other part of Tunisia.

9. ☐ The Mejerda River Valley contains very old villages with olive, almond, and pomegranate orchards.

10. ☐ There are two groups of mountains found in Tunisia.

11. ☐ All the rivers in Tunisia dry up during the hot season.

12. ☐ Along the coast of Tunisia are many good harbors and sandy beaches.

Learning About Tunisia's Climate

A. Reproduce "Student Activity 7: Tunisia's Climate" for your students.

B. Have your students read the information as a large group or as an independent reading activity. Discuss Tunisia's climate with your students. Compare Tunisia's climate with the climate in their country. Note the similarities and differences. Explain that Tunisia is closer to the equator and has a warmer climate.

C. Reproduce the "Student Activity 8: Tunisia's Climate" worksheet for your students. The students are to record the answers to the questions on the lines provided using words from the information.

Answer Key:

1. southern Tunisia
2. 12 hours
3. January to March
4. a hot, dry dusty wind from the Sahara Desert
5. Mediterranean climate
6. central Tunisia
7. mild, sunny winters and hot, dry summers
8. autumn
9. 50°C (122°F)
10. 10 days

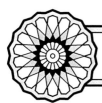

Tunisia's Climate

The weather in Tunisia is usually warm and sunny all year. Sometimes it rains in certain places during the winter months.

In northern Tunisia and along its coastal regions, the people enjoy a Mediterranean climate. This type of climate has mild to warm, sunny winters and hot, dry summers. Some rain does fall during the winter. During the early summer and autumn, rain sometimes falls in heavy downpours. Rain mainly falls in the hills and mountains and they may receive 600 mm (24 in.) to 900 mm (32 in.) of rain. Snow falls for about 10 days higher up in the mountains.

In central Tunisia, the rainfall is less. Winter temperatures may drop quite low and frosts may occur. Summer temperatures are higher than on the coast. During the summer, which takes place during the months of June through to September, the weather is quite warm. August is usually the hottest month of the year. Temperatures may be as high as 31°C (88°F).

In southern Tunisia, the climate becomes drier and summer temperatures can rise very high. If rain occurs, in the spring and autumn, it can be very heavy. Usually this area is very dry and doesn't receive much rain.

Sand dunes in the hot Sahara Desert

Daily sunshine lasts as long as 12 hours during the summer months and seven to eight hours during the winter months. Winter takes place from January to March. Spring is April to June and spring wildflowers can be seen. Summer takes place from July to September and autumn falls during October to December.

In the spring, a very hot, dry, and dusty wind bringing air from the Sahara Desert can affect any part of the country. This wind is called a "chili" and makes temperatures rise as high as 50°C (122°F). This extreme temperature can make people extremely tired and sick. This type of extreme weather does not happen all the time. For most of the year Tunisia has a healthy, pleasant climate.

Tunisia's Climate

Did you enjoy reading about the climate in my country?

How well do you remember the facts that you learned?

> Answer each question with the correct word or words. Use the information to check your answers.

1. Where in Tunisia is the climate very dry and the temperatures quite high?
   _____

2. How much sunshine does Tunisia receive during the summer months each day?
   _____

3. At what time of the year does Tunisia have winter?
   _____

4. What is a "chili"?
   _____

5. What type of climate is enjoyed by the people living along the coast of Tunisia?
   _____

6. In which area of Tunisia does the temperature drop quite low causing frost to occur?
   _____

7. What is a Mediterranean climate?
   _____

8. During which season are the seas warm and the sun golden in Tunisia?
   _____

9. If a "chili" does occur in Tunisia, how high may the temperature get?
   _____

10. For how long does it snow in the mountains in northern Tunisia?
    _____

Lifestyles in Tunisia

Tunisian People and Family Life

A. Record the word "population" on the chalkboard. Discuss its meaning with your students. (**number of people living in a land**) What is the population of your country? Take estimated guesses from your students. Record them on the chalkboard. Then record the actual population of your country on the chalkboard. Have your students read the number and then compare their estimates with the actual population. Circle the closest estimate. Discuss the size of your country and if there is space for more people.

B. Relay the following information about Tunisia to your students. Tunisia's population is 10,276,158 (2007) people. Compare the population of Tunisia to the population of your country. Which country has the largest population? (**Answers may vary.**) Which country has the largest land size? (**Your country.**) Compare Tunisia's land size and population to other countries that you have studied. Are they the same size, larger, or smaller than Tunisia?

C. Discuss the people and their lifestyle in your own country in North America. Make a list of the things that contribute to their lifestyle such as customs, traditions, food, clothing, literature, music, art, celebrations, etc. Explain that all these aspects of their lifestyle contribute to the culture of their country.

Use the following information to help you introduce the lifestyle of the Tunisian people and their family life to your students.

Tunisian People and Family Life

Tunisian Arabs live in Tunisia, Libya, and France. Many of them live in their homeland, Tunisia. The Arab Tunisian culture has been greatly influenced by the culture of Arabs, Berbers, and the French. The Tunisian Arab population has three main characteristics. There is a large middle class which is very unusual in an Arabic culture, an extremely youthful population, and a unique Tunisian Arabic language which is used daily.

Tunisian people share similar values and beliefs and come from a similar background. It is said that modern Tunisia is fairly homogenous although Tunisians have blended many cultures such as Berbers, Phoenicians, Jews, Romans, Vandals, and Arabs over the centuries. This blending has created a unique Tunisian cultural identity. Modern Tunisians think of themselves as Arabs but are proud of their cultural heritage. On the island of Jerba and in communities along the edge of the Sahara Desert there are Berber people living still today.

Lifestyles in Tunisia

Language:

Arabic is the official language of Tunisia but there are also many varieties or dialects used by the people. Classical Arabic is used in the Qur'an. Modern literary Arabic is the language used by the government, the media, and in schools. Most Tunisians speak a mixture of modern literary Arabic and a Tunisian dialect of Arabic.

French is also spoken because at one time Tunisia was a French colony that belonged to France. The French language is mainly used for business. The third language spoken is English. The tourist industry and foreign investment has increased its usage in Tunisia. Berber-speaking people are only one percent of the population and their Berber language "Chelha" is only used and heard in remote villages.

Tunisian Society:

The Tunisian society is divided between the interior areas and the coastal areas. At one time the nomadic peoples lived in the interior areas of Tunisia. These areas were undeveloped regions compared to the areas on the lengthy coastline. The people who lived in coastal cities and towns tended to be better educated, wealthier, and more modern in their thinking and attitudes. The people who lived in the interior were poorer and lived more traditional lives.

The people along the coast lived in prosperous trading communities and farming villages. The ports had more contact with the outside world through trade. They were also able to exchange skills, knowledge, and customs. These people became much more modern in their thinking. Craftsmen shared the skills of their trades with others. Farms in the north were productive and farmers often owned their own land and were able to live well. The nomadic herders and farmers have changed very little over the centuries in the interior of Tunisia.

In recent years Tunisia's economy has improved and the standard of living for many urban Tunisians has improved. There is a large middle class in the Tunisian society that is not present in other North African communities and as a result large numbers of people have gone to live in the coastal cities in search of a better way to live and for work. Many of these rural Tunisians are forced to live in shantytowns called "gourbivilles" outside the cities. These Tunisians are very like the rural people and are more traditional in their thinking about Islam and the Arab world. Tunisia's economic growth has not changed the lives of rural Tunisians as much.

There are four main socioeconomic groupings in Tunisian society. These divisions have existed in Tunisian culture for centuries. In the top division are the old families who can trace their ancestry back to the original Arab

Lifestyles in Tunisia

conquerors of Tunisia. The second division has the members of the upper middle class which is made up of Western-educated professionals, politicians, businessmen, and large landowners. The third division is the middle class who are teachers, small business owners, shopkeepers, independent farmers, and skilled workers. The fourth division is made up of farm workers, poor farmers, and the unemployed.

After Tunisia gained its independence in 1956, its population grew. As a result, Tunisia had a large population of young people who were looking for jobs in the 1980s. At this time, Tunisia's economy was not doing very well and these young, educated Tunisians could not find work in their fields. Unhappy with their situation, many emigrated to Europe to find work. Even today, qualified professional people find it difficult to find work in their career.

Family Life:

Family life is a very important element of Tunisian society. Tunisians have a strong sense of family honor. Their social life and sense of identity centers on the family. Many families still include grandparents, parents, and children especially in many rural areas.

In Tunisia today, young people who are educated have challenged the role of the family in Tunisia. Young women desire more freedom of choice and want to marry someone they love, not someone the family chooses. The Tunisian family is now becoming a nuclear one consisting of a father, mother, and their children. Family traditions are still strong and the extended families still give a great deal of financial and emotional support.

In a Muslim society, marriage is the foundation of family life. It is important for a Muslim woman to marry as soon as she can so she can have children. Children give a woman status and security. Fathers of the bride and groom arrange the marriage. Marriage in a Muslim society is usually a family choice not a personal one. In rural communities arranged marriages are still quite common.

Young, educated people choose their own marriage partners and usually discuss their choice with their parents or marriage partnerships are made by arrangement between families. Girls are not supposed to marry someone beneath them and often marry cousins who are equal in status. Sometimes mothers search for brides for their sons during their visit to the public baths. Once an engagement is settled on, the families visit each other. The couple are showered with gifts. The marriage ceremony is quite simple. It involves the moving of the bride from her home to the groom's home while the groom waits outside. Once the bride and all her belongings are settled into the bridal chamber, the groom may enter and the couple are left alone for a period of time to get to know one another.

Lifestyles in Tunisia

The family household in Tunisia is based on the patriarchal family. The father is the dominant head. The mother cares for the children and their home. Tunisian social life revolves around the family and eating meals together is very important. The biggest meal of the day is lunch. Often friends and family members visit at this meal. Men often go to restaurants and coffee and tea houses with friends.

Tunisian Men and Women:

In a traditional Muslim society a man may have as many as four wives. A Muslim husband has a great deal of control over his wives and can divorce one by simply saying "I repudiate thee". A Muslim wife has no rights, no money, and her children belong to her husband. This custom is not an Islamic religious law but a cultural tradition of Arab tribes on the Arabian Peninsula that made men to be the head of the family and even the tribe. The ancient Berber tribes in Tunisia had different values. They felt women could be the head of a family or a tribe.

In order to protect women's rights in Tunisia "The Code of Personal Status" was adopted. These laws changed the position of women in a Muslim society. Men and women were made equal before the law. It abolished polygamy, granted both spouses the right to request a divorce, and established the minimum age for marriage for girls at 17 years providing they agreed to the marriage. As a result of this law, Tunisian women are more independent and are more able to pursue their own careers than women in other Islamic countries.

In an Islamic culture, there is a clear difference between the public world of men and the domestic world of women. There is a definite difference in what men and women can do according to traditional Muslim life. Many Tunisian men and women talk and work together in public at universities, the work place, on public transportation, and at social events. This interaction is far greater than in other Arab societies. Tunisian women are more involved in the public world of work and have careers as lawyers, doctors, teachers, and businesswomen.

Even though Tunisian women have made great advances in their public identity many do not have careers outside their homes. Many women are better educated than those in the past but they still spend their lives engaged in traditional family tasks such as raising children, cooking meals, and looking after their family's needs. Even though the new laws grant Tunisian women many freedoms, many people feel that the proper role of women in an Islamic society should be upheld. Some people feel that women should be encouraged to practice older Muslim customs. Some Muslim men resent the fact that women can hold the same job as they can.

Lifestyles in Tunisia

D. Discuss the following aspects of the culture of Tunisian people with your students:

- the different cultures that have affected the Tunisian people
- the Tunisian people
- the different languages spoken
- main areas inhabited by Tunisians
- how Tunisian Society is divided
- types of family life (traditional and nuclear)
- marriage
- the position of men and women in Tunisian society

Use the following questions to check your students listening skills during a discussion and lesson. The students should be able to supply the answers.

1. In what other countries do Tunisian Arabs live? **(Libya, France)**

2. What other cultures have had an effect on Tunisian culture? **(Phoenicians, Jews, Romans, Vandals, Arabs, French)**

3. What is the main language spoken in Tunisia? **(Arabic)**

4. What other languages may be heard? **(French, English, Berber)**

5. Which area in Tunisia is the most prosperous? **(the coast)**

6. Why were the coastal areas more prosperous than the interior areas of Tunisia? **(people better educated, had trades, wealthier, traded with other countries, more modern in their thinking)**

7. What was life like in the inland areas? **(people were poor, lived traditional lives)**

8. Why did people leave the inland areas to live in cities on the coast? **(wanted a better way of life and work)**

9. What is a gourbiville? **(a shanty town outside a city)**

10. What are the four groups in a Tunisian society? **(old families are the highest level; upper middle class; middle class; poor)**

11. Why did young, educated people go to live in other countries? **(couldn't find jobs in their career)**

12. Describe a traditional Tunisian family. **(parents, grandparents, children)**

13. Describe a nuclear family in Tunisia. **(mother, father, children)**

14. How do young people get married in a traditional Tunisian family? **(Fathers of the bride and groom arrange the marriage.)**

Lifestyles in Tunisia

15. How do young people get married in a modern Tunisian family? (**Young people choose who they want to marry and discuss their choice with their parents.**)

16. How have women's rights in Tunisia been protected? (**Laws were passed to protect their rights.**)

17. What were some of these laws? (**Men and women were made equal. A man can only have one wife. A husband or wife can request a divorce. A girl must be 17 years of age in order to get married and she must agree to it.**)

18. Why were these laws so important? (**Women in Tunisia are free to get an education and to find work. Women in other Islamic countries are not.**)

E. Reproduce "Student Activity 9: Tunisian Etiquette" for your students.

F. Have your students read the information as a large group activity or as an independent activity. Discuss the different customs and forms of etiquette practiced in Tunisia. Have your students find the ones practiced in their country.

G. Reproduce the "Student Activity 10: Tunisian Etiquette" worksheet for your students. The students are to choose five customs not practiced in their country and to record them on the lines provided.

H. Reproduce "Student Activity 11: Living in Tunisia" for your students.

I. Have your students read about the homes people build in rural Tunisia. Use this activity as a large group activity or as an independent one. Discuss the ways Tunisian people live in Tunisia. Have your students locate the answers to the following questions using the information.

   1. What are the three main materials used to build a home in the country in Tunisia? (**stone, adobe, concrete**)

   2. Why do you think the people paint their homes white? (**white reflects the heat keeping the house cool**)

   3. How big are the homes out in the country? (**one-storey high, one room inside**)

   4. Why are the roofs on most Tunisian homes flat? (**The roof is used as an outdoor sitting room.**)

   5. What would the inside of a Tunisian home look like? (**decorated with blue and yellow mosaic tiles; pillows and carpets on the floor**)

Lifestyles in Tunisia

6. Why do people live in tents in Tunisia? **(People were once herders and moved about.)**

7. What do you think it would be like to live in a tent as a home? **(Answers may vary.)**

8. How were Berber people clever when they built a home? **(Answers may vary.)**

9. Where do Berber people live? **(in caves or underground homes)**

10. What are the advantages of living in an underground home? **(Temperature is always the same. Cave stays warm when it gets cold outside. Cave stays cool when it gets hot. It is a safe place to live.)**

11. What do you think the disadvantages would be of living in an underground home? **(Answers may vary.)**

12. Why do you think the streets in the old parts of Tunisian cities are narrow, hilly, and winding? **(Answers may vary.)**

13. What part of a Tunisian city is called the "medina"? **(the oldest part)**

14. What part of a city is called the "ville nouveau"? **(the newest part)**

15. Where in a city is the section called the "gourbiville"? **(outside the city)**

16. What is a "gourbiville"? **(a shantytown; people live in makeshift houses; poorest section of the city)**

J. Reproduce the "Student Activity 12: Living in Tunisia" worksheet for your students. The students are to classify the information in each sentence as to what it is describing. It may be something seen in the country or in the city in Tunisia. The students are to record the word "city" or the word "country" on the lines provided.

1. country	2. city
3. country	4. city
5. country	6. city
7. country	8. city
9. city	10. country

Tunisian Etiquette

Tunisians are polite, respectful people. We always use our best manners when we are with family and friends.

Read about the ways in which we use our good manners.

Did you know that:

- Tunisians always treat people with respect while talking to them.

- Tunisians always show interest in another person's family during a greeting.

- Tunisian men always shake hands with each other when they meet.

- A Tunisian man will not shake the hand of a woman if she doesn't extend her hand first.

- Tunisian men will kiss each other on the cheeks if they haven't seen each other for a long time.

- Tunisian men and women never kiss one another in public.

- Tunisian men eat and shake hands with their right hand.

- Young Tunisian men and women do not date until they are ready for marriage.

- Tunisian men must show respect for each other.

- Tunisian men do not smoke in front of their fathers.

- Tunisians bring gifts of nuts, fruits, candy, or flowers when visiting someone's home.

- Tunisians always remove their shoes before entering a house.

- Tunisian women often cover their head and body with a cloth called a "safsari".

- A Tunisian man is not to carry his child in front of his father.

- Tunisian women only leave the house to go to places that are approved by her family.

- Tunisian men do not visit each other in their homes because the women would be present.

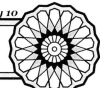

Tunisian Etiquette

 Some of the manners that you use in your country may be the same as the ones used in my country. Some may be quite different.

On the lines below record five Tunisian customs that are different from the customs in your country.

Illustrate one of the customs in the box.

Living in Tunisia

Tunisian people live in cities along the coast or in villages and farming communities inland.

Read the information and find out about the different types of homes seen in Tunisia.

Inside a wealthy Tunisian home

roof of the house is usually flat and is used as an outdoor sitting room in the evening when it is cooler. Some roofs are vaulted and are covered with rust-colored tiles. The inside of the homes are often decorated with blue and yellow mosaic tiles. There is very little furniture in each home. People often sit on carpets or cushions on the floors. These homes provide the people with a cool shelter from the strong sun.

In rural areas near the desert, many families live in tents called "gourbi". These tents are set up permanently and often form villages for people who were once herders of the desert.

The people in Tunisia live in a variety of different homes. Tunisian homes vary from region to region. In rural areas, the homes are small, one-storey houses of white-washed stone, adobe, or concrete. The houses are usually one-room dwellings. The doors and window frames are often painted green or blue. The

Traditional Berber store rooms

Living in Tunisia

In southern Tunisia, Berbers build dwellings carved out of rock. Matmâta is a cave village located on the slope of a hill. Berber people have been digging their homes out of the ground for more than a thousand years in Matmâta. In this village there are 100 underground homes and even an underground hotel.

Inside a cave house in Matmâta, Tunisia

Underground homes are very useful places in hot dry climates. Under the ground, the temperature is always the same. At night, when the desert gets cold, the cave stays warm and comfortable. During the day when the sun is extremely hot, the caves are cool.

Cave homes are built around artificial craters that are 5 to 10 meters (16-32 feet) deep with doors and windows in the steep walls towards the crater. The crater looks like a patio and the lower part of the wall is often painted white. Sometimes craters are connected by various tunnels. Most of the houses are a single crater with several rooms used for living, sleeping or storing food. The interior of the cave home is usually whitewashed. A sloping tunnel leads into the underground home or a ladder is used which can be removed in time of danger.

Most of Tunisia's cities are ancient and have been built by many different cultures. In Tunisia's cities luxury homes and apartment buildings are lived in by the rich and middle-class Tunisians. The front doors of houses open directly on to the street. There are no front yards and very few windows. Most single family homes are small. Many houses are two to three storeys high. The houses have flat roofs that are used as outdoor living space.

Souse, a city in Tunisia

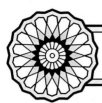

Living in Tunisia

Years ago, cities in Tunisia were divided into quarters or sections. The people living in each quarter were of the same religion or culture. Houses were made of brick or mud-brick. The walls, doors, and ceilings were decorated. Wooden shutters, doors, and window sashes were painted a bright blue. This section of the city is called the "medina".

A house on the beach in Tunisia

A street in a medina

In the medina, streets are narrow, winding, steep, and made of stone. This is the old section of a Tunisian city. This area is usually filled with old, historical buildings, older homes, and monuments.

Another section in a Tunisian city is called the "ville nouvelle". This is the newer part of the city that was built by the French. In this area the buildings are more modern and the streets are wider.

The poorest section of a city is on the outside of it. This section is called "gourbivilles" or shanty towns. The people live in makeshift houses without running water and toilets. Many people hope that they will not have to live in the gourbiville for very long. They hope that they will some day have enough money to become part of the middle-class society in Tunisia. Unfortunately some families have lived here for generations.

Name: _____

Living in Tunisia

The homes we have in Tunisia provide us with a cool place away from the hot sun and the heat during the day.

Match each sentence to the place where you may see it in Tunisia

Would you see it in the city or out in the country in Tunisia? Record the word **city** or the word **country** on the line provided.

1. The house was a one-room dwelling made out of adobe bricks that had been white-washed. _____

2. The tourists were taking pictures of old buildings and statues that they had found in the medina. _____

3. The family sat in their cool underground home away from the heat of the afternoon. _____

4. Rich and middle-class Tunisians live in beautiful homes and large apartments in Tunisia. _____

5. Arafat, a young Berber boy, lived in a large colorful tent called a gourbi on the edge of an oasis in the desert. _____

6. The front door of each house on Mona's street opened directly on to the busy street. _____

7. We noticed that the underground home had several rooms that were connected by tunnels. _____

8. We were surprised to see so many modern buildings and such wide streets on our visit to Tunis. _____

9. In the medina, the streets were narrow, hilly, winding, and hard to walk on during our trip. _____

10. It was scary climbing down the wooden ladder so we could visit the home in a crater. _____

Tunisia's Economy

Work of the People

A. Review the following terms with your students: economy, trade, import, export, and balance of trade.

B. Discuss Tunisia's economy with your students.

Explain the following points to your students at a level they will understand.

- After 50 years of independence Tunisia has changed from a poor country to a middle income nation.
- Tunisia has a healthy growing economy.
- Tunisia has a bright economic outlook.

C. How can such a small country with such a large population have a growing economy?

- Its economy once depended mainly on agriculture but now has other industries such as mining, energy, tourism, and manufacturing.
- Tunisia has been able to attract other countries to invest in their country such as Europe, Japan, and the United States.
- Tunisia has a good working system which ensures that goods can be transported quickly and cheaply. It has a good highway system and six major seaports.
- Tunisia was ranked as the most competitive country in Africa.
- Tunisia has a good political climate and a stable society that investors like.
- The Tunisian government offers foreign investors special exemptions on taxes and customs.
- Tunisia has had strong leaders who were interested in seeing the country get stronger.

D. Even though Tunisia has a good economy it does have one major problem and that is high unemployment. Many people who are well educated in their field cannot find work in Tunisia. Many leave the country to work in other countries in Europe and send money home to help their families.

E. Make a list of the following industries that provide work for Tunisian people on the chalkboard.

- Agriculture or Farming
- Fishing
- Mining
- Energy
- Manufacturing
- Tourism

Discuss each area with your students using the information and activity sheets provided.

Tunisia's Economy

F. Reproduce "Student Activity 13: Farming in Tunisia" for your students.

Use this information sheet as a large group reading activity or as an independent reading activity.

Discuss the ways Tunisians farm. Compare their methods to the ones used in your country.

G. Reproduce the "Student Activity 14: Farming in Tunisia" worksheet for your students. Direct your students to complete each activity carefully.

Answer Key:

1. by hand; old fashioned way; traditional way
2. government-owned land
3. **Man's Jobs:** plants crops; digs pits and cisterns; irrigates the land; harvests crops; herds the animals
   Woman's Jobs: hoes and weeds the crops; cares for animals; spins, weaves wool; makes couscous; preserves fruits and vegetables; manages the household
4. men away working somewhere else
5. almonds, beef, citrus fruits, dairy products, dates, grain, olive oil, olives, sugar beets, tomatoes

H. Reproduce "Student Activity 15: The Date Palm Tree" for your students.

Use this information sheet as a large group reading activity or as an independent reading activity.

Discuss the importance of this tree to the Tunisian people in the past and today.

I. Reproduce the "Student Activity 16: The Date Palm Tree" worksheet for your students. Direct the students to use the information sheet to complete the activity.

Answer Key:

1. It loves a hot, dry climate and does well in a desert oasis where few plants grow.
2. They provide shade, food, building materials, and fuel.
3. They are eaten fresh or dried.
4. A strong rope is made from the fiber in the bark.
5. A date palm grows as tall as 30 meters (100 feet).
6. Dates grow in clusters at the end of stalks.
7. The date has thick, sweet flesh that is covered by tough skin and inside the date is a single, large seed.
8. One tree can grow 45 kilograms (100 pounds) of fruit each year for 60 years.

Tunisia's Economy

J. Reproduce "Student Activity 17: Industry in Tunisia" for your students.

Use this information sheet as a group reading activity or as an independent reading activity.

Discuss the different types of industries found in Tunisia. Compare them to industries found in your country.

K. Reproduce the "Student Activity 18: Industry in Tunisia" worksheet for your students. Direct your students to answer each question with a complete sentence.

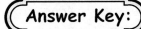

Answer Key:

1. manufacturing
2. iron and phosphates
3. to make fertilizers
4. people make low wages, cheaper
5. fish, fruit, vegetables, olive oil, sugar, flour
6. in small workshops
7. has many tourists attractions and beaches
8. a local market in Tunisia

L. Bring the following information pertaining to Tunisia's economy to your students' attention .

  • Coastal regions are far more developed than inland regions.

  • People who live inland are poorer than those on the coast.

  • The gap between the rich and the poor is growing wider.

  • Poor people resent the rich who have great fortunes.

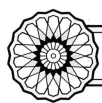

Farming in Tunisia

Farming in Tunisia has always been a very important industry. People need food in order to live.

Read the information and find out how we farm in Tunisia.

In Tunisia, farming is an important way of life. Many farmers raise animals or grow crops on small rented or family-owned farms. The farmers on small farms do most of the work by hand and use animals to pull plows to cultivate the land. Old-fashioned methods are used for most things. In some areas, farmers work on government-owned land and use machinery and modern methods.

In many farming areas, the people live in flat-roofed houses with thick adobe walls to keep out the intense heat. In mountain areas, homes are made of stucco or stone. The homes are simply furnished and do not have running water or telephones.

A rural village

*This Tunisian well uses animal power
to lift water out of the ground*

Farming in Tunisia

In Tunisia's farming regions, the people follow a traditional way of life. In a family household, the men are responsible for bringing money into the house either by farming or by having another job. The women are responsible for managing the household and all household duties such as cooking, cleaning, and collecting water and wood. Women often have to run the farm if the men are away working at another job to make money. Women often work on large farms and get paid half the money that the men make.

harvesting the crops, and herding the animals. The women are responsible for hoeing and weeding the crops and caring for the animals kept near the house. They also process the raw materials produced by the farm into useful items by spinning and weaving the wool from sheep, preparing couscous from wheat, and preserving fruit and vegetables.

Farms in Tunisia produce olives, olive oil, grain, tomatoes, citrus fruits, sugar beets, dates, almonds, beef, and dairy products. Sheep are raised for their meat and wool.

Olive trees

Olives on the branch

On a Tunisian farm, men are responsible for preparing the land for planting crops, digging pits and cisterns (a structure that holds rain water), irrigating the fields,

Farming in Tunisia

Farming is an important industry in my country. Many different kinds of crops are grown to feed our people.

Complete each following activity carefully and neatly.

1. How is farming done in Tunisia?
   _____
   _____

2. Where are modern farming methods used in Tunisia?
   _____
   _____

3. On the following chart list the responsibilities that a Tunisian man and woman have on their farm.

Man's Jobs	Woman's Jobs
_____	_____
_____	_____
_____	_____
_____	_____

4. Why do Tunisian women often run the farm alone?
   _____
   _____

5. List the things that Tunisian farms produce in alphabetical order. Circle the ones that are not produced in your country.
   _____
   _____
   _____
   _____

The Date Palm Tree

Did you know that people who lived 5,000 years ago in Tunisia grew date palm trees? It is one of the oldest crop plants in the world.

Read the information about this marvelous tree.

The date palm tree grows in Tunisia. It loves a hot, dry climate and does well on a desert oasis where few plants can grow. The fruit of this tree is an important part of the diet of Tunisian people. Muslim people believe the date palm represents the tree of life which is described in one of their legends.

Date palms are used for many different things. They provide shade, food, building materials, and fuel. Dates are rich in sugar and provide energy that people need. They are eaten fresh or dried. Dried dates are used in cooking and can be easily stored and preserved. The trunk and leaves of a date palm are used as building materials. A strong rope is made from the fiber in the bark. Its leaves are used to make baskets and mats and other useful things. Even the pits inside the dates are burned as fuel or ground up to be used to feed animals.

A grove of date palms

Dates ripening on the tree

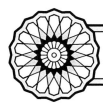

The Date Palm Tree

A date palm grows as tall as 30 meters (100 feet). Its trunk is straight and rough and its base and top are the same thickness. Feather-like leaves that are 3 to 6 meters (10 to 20 feet) long fan out from the top of the trunk. Date palm trees usually grow in clumps.

Dates grow in clusters at the end of stalks. One cluster may hold 600 to 1,700 dates at the time of picking. Date palms produce a lot of fruit. One tree can grow 45 kilograms (100 pounds) of fruit each year for 60 years.

Between February and June flowers bloom on the trees. The fruit ripens from June to December. The date is an oblong fruit that measures 2.5 centimeters to 5 centimeters (1 to 2 inches) in length. The date has thick, sweet flesh that is covered by tough skin and inside the date is a single, large seed. Dates may be yellow to orange, red, or green in color depending on the kind.

Fresh dates

Date palms require warm temperatures and dry air to ripen properly. The roots need a regular supply of water that may be supplied by irrigation or an underground spring. Workers harvest the clusters of dates by hand. The dates are sprayed to kill the insects and then placed in a warm place to ripen more and to dry.

Dried dates

The Date Palm Tree

The date palm tree is a very interesting plant. Tunisians have eaten the fruit from this tree for centuries.

Locate a sentence in the information that answers each of the following questions. Record the sentence on the lines provided.

1. Where do date palm trees grow?

   _____
   _____

2. What are the four main uses for date palm trees?

   _____
   _____

3. How are dates usually eaten?

   _____
   _____

4. What is made from the bark of a date palm tree?

   _____
   _____

5. How tall can a date palm grow?

   _____
   _____

6. How do dates grow on a date palm tree?

   _____
   _____

7. What does a date look like?

   _____
   _____

8. How much fruit can a date palm tree grow in a year?

   _____
   _____

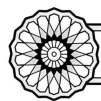

Industry in Tunisia

Even though Tunisia is a small country we have many different industries. Our factories make many things that our people need and some things are exported to other countries.

Once Tunisia gained its independence from France, it began to develop a variety of industries in its country to provide jobs for its people. Many new industries were created in the areas of agriculture, mining, energy, and manufacturing.

In 1960, the oil industry was developed when petroleum was discovered in the south of Tunisia. Natural gas has been discovered and has created work for the people as well.

Tunisia has a good mining industry which produces iron ore and phosphates that are used in fertilizers. Tunisia is the world's largest source of phosphates. Most of the country's phosphate mines are found in the central and southwest regions of the country. Many factories make fertilizer using phosphates.

The manufacturing industry is the most important one in Tunisia. It has factories that make clothing, shoes, and leather goods. Many foods are processed in factories such as flour milling. Fish, fruit, and vegetables are canned. Olive oil is made and sugar is refined.

Fresh pressed olive oil

Other factories make mechanical and electrical products, building materials, and rubber products. Tunisia now has 60 automobile assembly plants. Tunisia has a highly skilled work force who work for low

49

Industry in Tunisia

wages. This has led many European clothing companies to choose Tunisia's factories to make their clothing.

For many years, Tunisians have been known for their handicrafts. These crafts are made in small workshops for the local markets called "souks" and for tourists. These workshops usually employ about 10 workers including the owner. The workers make clothing, rugs, pottery, copper and leather goods, jewelry, and embroidered articles. These handicrafts are exported to other countries or sold to the tourists. The city of Kairouan is famous for its carpets.

A Tunisian hotel

Throughout the country of Tunisia and in the many cities and towns are weekly markets that provide goods for the people to buy. Food, clothing, household goods, and animals are sold at markets called "souks". Many poor people are street vendors who sell goods that they make on the streets and roads.

Tunisian carpets

The tourist industry is steadily growing and this helps Tunisia's economy in many ways. Major tourist attractions such as the beautiful beaches along the east coast, Jerba Island, the oases in the Tunisian Sahara Desert, and the many ruins of old cities attract people from all over the world.

A handicraft shop in a souk

Industry in Tunisia

We are proud of the way that our country is growing. There are many different kinds of factories that make goods for us and other countries.

| Answer each of the following questions. |

1. Which industry in Tunisia is the most important?

   _____

2. What are the names of the minerals found in Tunisia?

   _____

3. What is the mineral phosphate used for?

   _____

4. Why are other countries using Tunisian factories to make things for them?

   _____

5. Which foods are processed in Tunisian factories?

   _____

   _____

6. Where are Tunisian crafts made?

   _____

   _____

7. Why is the tourist industry growing in Tunisia?

   _____

   _____

8. What is a "souk"?

   _____

Tunisia's Culture

A. The following information has been provided for the teacher for support during lessons and discussions on the various aspects of Tunisian culture. The information deals with religion, clothing, food, holidays and celebrations, and arts and crafts.

B. Worksheets accompany each aspect of Tunisian culture and may be used as follow-ups to lessons.

Tunisian Language and Education:

Tunisia's official language is Arabic and many of its dialects are spoken around the country. The Muslim holy book called the Qur'an is written in classical Arabic. The language used by the government is a form of classical Arabic called modern literary Arabic. French is also spoken and is used during business. English is used with foreign investors and with tourists. A small percentage of the population who are Berber speak "Chelha", which is the Berber language.

The government of Tunisia feels it is very important that everyone in Tunisia has the right to go to school. It is one of the government's top priorities. Before Tunisia's independence only a few people received any education. Many Tunisian parents had to be persuaded that education is important for their children and for the growth of the country. In the poorer, more traditional and agricultural areas, education does not always seem important. Parents feel children are more useful at home looking after flocks of sheep or helping out on the land.

By law, children in Tunisia must attend school between the ages of six to 16. Preschool is offered to children from the ages of three to six but this is optional and parents must agree to pay the fee. Children attend primary schools between the ages of six and 12. Lessons are conducted in Arabic and French is taught from the third or fourth year. At the end of the sixth year in primary school, children take an examination. Students must pass this examination in order to go on to the preparatory level of education.

Children from the ages of 12 to 14 attend preparatory schools. Here they are taught in Arabic and French. Some students may even attend special training centers. High school is only available to pupils from the ages of 14 to 18 and those who have passed the basic schooling examination and have a basic schooling certificate. During the first year of high school all students take the same subjects. The following three years are for specialization. After high school students may attend universities, colleges, or technical institutes.

People who are educated stand out amongst the Tunisian population because they can speak more than one language and are able to hold specialized jobs.

Tunisia's Culture

Today more and more children living in poor interior areas are able to learn to read and write because schools are being built in rural areas. School begins every year after summer vacation and newspapers report stories about children going back to school and interview children about how they feel about starting school again. Everything is being done to promote education and its importance.

Tunisia's Religions:

Most Tunisians are Muslim and belong to the Sunni school of Islam. One percent are Christians and one percent are Jewish. Years ago Tunisia was an important center for Islamic learning. The Zitouna Mosque in Tunis was the main place for Islamic studies and more than 20,000 Islamic schools or "madrasas" were in operation throughout Tunisia.

The "umma" is the community of believers in Islam. This community is very large and believers are found in many countries around the world. They are found in the Middle East, North Africa, Southeast Asia, North America, and Europe. In Islam, there are two main branches called the Sunni and the Shia. Each branch does not believe the "umma" should be led in the same way. Most Tunisia's Muslims belong to the Sunni branch that also has the most believers in the world.

Islam is practiced by the majority of Tunisians and it governs their personal, economic, and legal lives. Islam came from what is today Saudi Arabia. The Prophet Muhammad is seen as the last of God's emissaries following in the footsteps of Jesus, Moses, and Abraham to bring revelation to mankind.

All Muslims share the same belief in the importance of the Five Pillars of Islam which states the responsibilities of prayer and faith. Muslims believe that they should behave ethically and do so by being generous, fair, honest, and respectful, especially in family relationships. Islam forbids adultery, gambling, usury, the eating of pork, and the drinking of alcohol. The Qur'an is the holy book of Islam, the "Hadith" are the sayings and teachings of Muhammad, and the "sunna" is the example of Muhammad's personal behavior. These three aspects of Islam form a guide to the spiritual, ethical, and social behavior for Sunni Muslims.

The Five Pillars of Islam are rules that all Muslims must follow. They are:

• Shahada - There is only one God and Muhammad was his last prophet. Islam also recognizes Abraham, Moses, and Jesus as prophets.

• Salat - This is the prayer performed five times a day in a special position. Prayers are said at sunrise, midday, afternoon, sunset, and evening. The

Tunisia's Culture

faithful must bow and face Mecca. The muezzin calls the people to prayer at the correct times.

- Zakat - This is the donations given to charity. Muslims are to give part of their income above what they need to build and maintain mosques and to help the poor.

- Sawm - This is the daytime fasting during the month of Ramadan. In Tunisia fasting is done if the person wishes to, and is not a state-enforced law.

- Hajj - This is the pilgrimage to Mecca. A Muslim is supposed to visit Mecca once in their lifetime during the 12th month of the lunar calendar.

The mosque is a building used for worship, a meeting place, and a place to study the Islamic religion. Usually a Muslim school is attached to the mosque where students can study the Islamic scriptures. Years ago a mosque had a building called a minaret attached to it. Five times a day the muezzin would climb the minaret to call the faithful to prayer. In Tunisia today the call to prayer is broadcast on radio and television, interrupting programming. Friday is the Muslim holy day for communal prayer. People do not work but attend prayer sessions at the mosque. The prayers can be lead by any adult man who knows the prayer forms. The man who regularly leads the prayers is called an "imam".

During prayers in a mosque on Friday, the imam faces the direction of Mecca. The men stand behind him and the women stand behind the men. Prayers are recited from the Qur'an and other phrases of praise to Allah. The people may bow from the hips or kneel with their faces to the ground. A sermon is said before the prayers.

Tunisian Clothing:

Clothing in a Muslim country is influenced by the climate, available materials, and cultural traditions which include social status, group identity, and religion. People who live in a warmer climate wear loose clothing to protect themselves from the sun and to keep cool. White or light colored clothing is cooler than dark clothing in the sunlight. Head coverings are worn for protection from the sun. Cotton fabrics are used for clothing that is worn during the hot weather. Wool is used for clothing worn during cooler weather. Camel hair is also woven into clothing for the cold weather. Some clothing is made out of plant fibers called linen. Silk is an expensive fabric that was imported from China, and is worn by only rich people.

Cultural traditions are also important in the style of clothing worn. Clothing shows the social status of its people. Married and single women might wear different clothing and head coverings. Young women nearing the age of marriage and married women would not wear the same type of clothing. Clothing worn by women outside the home is different from

Tunisia's Culture

clothing worn inside the home. Different situations affect the type of clothing worn. Clothing used for working in the fields would be different from clothing worn to a mosque.

All clothing worn by Muslim people is dictated by the Qur'an and the sayings of the Prophet Muhammad. In the Qur'an, men and women were told to be modest in their dress. Modest clothing for a woman is a head covering called a "hijab". Whenever a woman entered a mosque she always covered her head. In some societies even the woman's face was covered. Men should not wear silk clothing or gold jewelry to show that they are rich. Clothing should not be worn to attract attention or be worn to show off. All parts of the body must be entirely covered and only the hands and face may be seen. The material used in clothing must not be so thin that it can be seen through. Clothing must be loose so that the shape of the body cannot be seen and shown off. Women's clothing must be different from men's clothing. Women should not artificially lengthen their hair with wigs or weaves nor should they have tattoos. A Muslim should not wear clothing to look like a non-Muslim. Men's robes or shirts should extend below the ankles but may not trail on the ground. While praying in a mosque, clothing should be plain and should not attract the attention of others. Men must wear their hair neatly cut a little below the ears.

In Tunisia today, people dress in a more modern fashion especially in the cities. Men are often seen dressed in business suits and women dressed in European style jostling their way through the rush hour crowds in busy cities. Some wear head coverings, some do not. Women, even the younger ones, will wear the traditional light white veil called the "sifsari". It is draped over the head, leaving the face free and then it is wrapped round the body to just above the ankles. The veil is often a practical piece of clothing and is popular during winter months when it is cooler and when dusty winds blow in the summer. Younger women will put it on when they want to go out without bothering to change their clothes or to put on their make-up.

Although Tunisians dress in western style clothing, traditional dress remains common in rural areas and villages. Many men wear a brimless hat called a "chichia". It is made of brown or red felt and is either rounded or flat on top. Traditional male clothing includes a "jalabiyya", a long dress-like garment and baggy pants. Women who dress traditionally wear the sifsari. In rural areas, women often wear a large, loose covering draped across their heads and shoulders called a "millia". Colorful necklaces, bracelets, anklets, and earrings are part of their everyday dress.

Tunisian Food:

Tunisian cooking is traditionally hot and spicy in taste. The Tunisians love their hot chilli peppers. The main staple of a Tunisian meal is couscous.

Tunisia's Culture

Couscous is a type of tiny pasta made from semolina wheat sprinkled with oil and water and then rolled into tiny grains. It is cooked in a special kind of double boiler called a couscousiere. Meat and vegetables are cooked in the bottom half and the couscous is cooked in the top half by the steam from the boiling food below. The steam also flavors the couscous. The meat and vegetables and juices are served over the couscous. Couscous is the North African version of rice, pasta, or potatoes eaten in other countries.

Kebabs of lamb or fish are common in Tunisia as well as sweet pastries stuffed with nuts and dates that have been soaked in honey. A sauce called "harissa" made from chopped red peppers, salt, and garlic softened in oil is usually on the table and can be added to everything – even soup.

A popular salad called "chakchouka" is made of tomatoes, onions, peppers, and hard-boiled eggs. "Michouia" is a main course of grilled tomatoes, peppers, and onions with olive oil, tuna, sliced hard-boiled eggs, lemon juice, and capers. "Shorba" is a soup made with meat or fish and is usually a meal in itself in Tunisia. Various kinds of roasts are prepared with herbs and spices.

Tunisians cook a variety of stews in a pot with a cone-shaped lid called a "tagine". Dishes made in this pot are called tagines as well. Spinach tagine consists of beans, beef, onions, tomato sauce, pepper, spinach, and egg. Other kinds of tagines make use of everything from chicken to prunes and honey.

An egg "brik" is a fast food sold at roadside stalls or served as the first course in Tunisian restaurants. The egg brik is a triangle of paper-thin pastry containing an egg along with chopped parsley and capers. The entire pastry is deep fried until the egg inside is cooked and the pastry is crisp. The egg brik is always eaten with the fingers and can be messy, leaving egg on your face.

Tunisians eat an abundance of local fish and fresh fruit. The fish and shellfish are cooked simply and taste very good. Fruit varies according to the season. Melons, grapes, peaches, figs, dates, pomegranates, and oranges are often served for dessert at the end of a meal.

Tunisians love to drink strong Turkish coffee and sweet mint tea served in glasses. Pork and alcohol are forbidden by the Islamic religious code.

Tunisian Celebrations:

Most celebrations and holidays in Tunisia are religious ones connected to Islam. Muslims have their own calendar which is based on the cycles of the moon. It has 12 months but only has 354 days unlike other calendars. This is why the Islamic New Year moves eleven days backwards through the seasons each year. "Murharram" is the first month of the Muslim year and its first day is celebrated as New Year's Day. When the new moon appears in the sky, people attend services at mosques and special prayers are said. They also pay

Tunisia's Culture

homage to the Prophet Muhammad. The most important part of the day is to tell or listen to the story of Muhammad's flight from Medina to Mecca. This story is also broadcast on the radio. Muslims are to think about how they are leading their lives and about their destiny. Some Muslims exchange New Year's cards and gifts on the Islamic New Year.

Sometime in April, the "Mouled" is held in Tunisia. This day is celebrated to remember the birthday of Muhammad. Families prepare a special pudding of sweetened sorghum, a grain much like corn, to share with friends and family. Sometimes a pastry called "assida" is made. It is made of semolina flour and topped with butter and honey and decorated with dried fruit and ground pistachio nuts.

Ramadan is the most important festival of the Islamic year. It falls during different seasons of the year due to the lunar calendar. During the holy month of Ramadan, all Muslims must fast from dawn to dusk and are only permitted to work six hours each day. Fasting includes no eating, drinking, cigarette smoking, or gum chewing from dawn until dusk. This is called "sawm".

Each evening, the Ramadan celebrations begin. Favorite dishes and desserts are served. People visit other families and prepare special meals. Wealthy families often entertain large gatherings. Before the end of Ramadan, Muslims are to share their good fortune with the poor and give money to their mosques.

Ramadan ends with the festival of "Eid al-Fitr" which means Feast of the Breaking of the Fast. At this festival, people dress in their finest clothes and decorate their homes with lights and other decorations. Treats, gifts, and new clothes are given to the children. Muslims visit family and friends during this three day celebration. Intense socializing and feasting takes place during this time.

"Eid al-Idha" or Feast of Sacrifice is the most important feast of the Muslim calendar. It lasts for three days and ends the Pilgrimage to Mecca. Eid al-Idha celebrates Ibraham's (Abraham's) willingness to obey Allah (God) by sacrificing his son Ishmael (Isaac) as told in the old Testament. According to the Qur'an, Ibraham was about to sacrifice his son when a voice from the sky stopped him and allowed him to sacrifice a ram instead. To celebrate Ibraham's willingness to obey and his dedication to Allah, sheep, goats, or camels are sacrificed to Allah and the meat is given to the poor and needy.

Tunisians enjoy life and celebrate it with festivals. Even the smallest village sets aside time to celebrate the summer, the harvest, the fishing season, a local saint, or the coming of spring. Visitors are always welcome at festivals and are encouraged to participate in the dancing and share a cup of mint tea.

Tunisia's Culture

The Palm Tree Festival in Tozeur involves local folk dancing and singing. Camel racing has proved to be popular with tourists. Many international music festivals are held during the summer in open air theaters throughout the country.

Tunisian Music and Dance:

Classical Arabic music does not use harmony. The music is sung or played in a solo or by a single musician. Sometimes a group of musicians repeat what the soloists sang or played but without harmony. There is no harmony because the soloist often improvises or makes up something different.

The rhythm of the music is played by tapping the center or edge of a drum or tambourine. Sometimes the rhythm is played in an exciting and complicated way. Musicians play stringed instruments that are plucked with the fingers or played with a bow. The "oud" is the most popular stringed instrument. It is similar to a guitar with five or six strings. The harp has about 12 strings or more. The strings are plucked with the fingers. The Persian fiddle has two strings and is played with a bow. The "sax" is a Turkish, long-necked lute. It has six strings. The "qanun" is the same shape as a trapezoid. It has 26 triple strings. The strings are plucked with short pieces of horn.

Musicians learn to play traditional music "by ear", by listening to others and then improvising or making changes. Traditional Arabic music was not written but was passed down in an apprentice system where the teacher shows the student.

Music is important to the people of Arabic countries. Common people participated in folk songs and dances. Arabic people love to sing and dance the ancient songs of the desert, love, the homeland, beauty, and nature. Poetry and music was closely tied and many of the great Arabic poems are related to the songs of nomadic tribes. Folk music was sung around campfires, in homes, and as part of celebrations such as weddings. Entertainers would travel from place to place to entertain in the towns and cities. This activity is still seen on the streets of Tunisian cities and towns.

Dancing in a Muslim country is viewed in different ways. Some Muslims feel there should be no dancing at all. They view dancing as moving towards sin. Others feel folk dancing just between men or just between women is fine but not between mixed couples or in front of the opposite sex. Many Muslims feel that the way dancing is done in North America is very wrong and sinful. On the other hand, some Muslims see music and dancing as a way to become closer to Allah.

Many traditional dances are done with separate groups of men and women but not mixed. Some of the folk dances celebrate the achievements of past

Tunisia's Culture

warriors, the planting season, the harvest, and the changes in the seasons. Others are done to celebrate rites of passage in a person's life such as weddings, birth, or circumcisions.

Tunisian Arts and Crafts:

Tunisian people have a fine tradition in making crafts. This ability is shown in the manufacture of textiles, leather goods (especially shoes), ceramics, glass, and furniture. Potters throughout Tunisia still make pots for everyday use in homes and the designs have changed little in the last two thousand years.

Women in villages and towns still make molded pots and spin and dye wool for the blankets that they weave. Carpets and rugs are woven out of wool as well. Mats are woven out of grass, and clothing is finely embroidered.

The government in Tunisia has taken an interest in the manufacture of home-made handicrafts as it was afraid these skills would die out and be forgotten. The Tunisian Handicrafts Board (ONAT) was established to control the quality of the crafts and to set up centers where these crafts could be taught to children and young adults.

Tunisian people excel in particular crafts. Nabeul is famous for its pottery and decorated ceramic tiles. Gafsa specializes in beautifully colored blankets. Jerba's dyed wools are made into woollen rugs and shawls. Delicately made wire bird cages are made in Sidi Bou. Other beautiful objects are made from olive wood, leather, beaten copper, and wrought iron. Beautiful silver jewelry is also made. The most sought after handicrafts by tourists are the handmade carpets of Kairouan.

The designs used by Tunisian women in their carpet-making, embroidery, and weaving are quite interesting. The Islam religion forbids any representation of the human form in any artwork. Sometimes the women who live in the Sahara Desert will weave human figures into their rugs. Trees, flowers, birds, and animals are usually used to decorate clothing, leather, ceramics, wood, and jewelry. Two favorite motifs are "khomsa" which is the open hand and the fish. Both are regarded as kindly, protective, and good luck signs.

C. Reproduce "Student Activity 19: Going to School in Tunisia" for your students. Have your students read the information as a large group activity or as an independent reading activity. Discuss the school system in Tunisia and compare its system with the one in your country noting the differences and similarities.

D. Reproduce the "Student Activity 20: Going to School in Tunisia" worksheet for your students. Have your students complete the activities using full sentence answers.

Tunisia's Culture

Answer Key:

1. Answers may vary.
2. to work on the farm and to look after the animals
3. The schools are overcrowded and grades must share the same classrooms.
4. read right to left
5. 29 letters; capitals used at the end of words and sentences; some letters are connected while some are not; small dashes and hooks are used above or below the letters

E. Reproduce "Student Activity 21: Religion in Tunisia" for your students. Have your students read the information as a large group activity or as an independent one. Discuss the Muslim religion practiced in Tunisia with your students.

F. Reproduce the "Student Activity 22: Religion in Tunisia" worksheet with your students. Students are to write meanings for the words that pertain to the Islamic faith.

Answers may vary but should contain the following basic meanings:

Answer Key:

1. minaret: a tower attached to a mosque
2. Islam: the Muslim religion based on the teachings of Muhammad
3. imam: the leader of a mosque
4. mosque: a building where Muslims worship
5. Mecca: the sacred city of Islam in Saudi Arabia where Muslims go on pilgrimages
6. Qur'an or Koran: the sacred book of the Muslims
7. Allah: Muslim word for God
8. Muhammad: a prophet of Allah or God
9. prophet: a religious man who teaches about things that have been revealed to him by Allah or God
10. muezzin: a man who calls Muslims to prayer five times a day

G. Reproduce "Student Activity 23: Tunisian Fashions" for your students. Have your students read the information as a large group activity or as an independent reading activity.

Discuss how climate, traditions, religion, and social position affect the way people dress in a Muslim country.

Discuss why Tunisians are more modern in their dress than other Muslim countries.

Tunisia's Culture

H. Reproduce the "Student Activity 24: Tunisian Fashions" worksheet for your students. The students are to research the names of Tunisian traditional dress on the Internet using a search engine such as Google. Their findings are to be recorded on the sheet.

Answer Key:

These are possible answers:

1. skull cap for men
2. long, woollen outer robe without sleeves or collar and closed by a single button worn by men
3. closed shoes worn by men and women
4. turban
5. wooden clogs worn by women in the baths
6. a pointed bonnet for women
7. a vest in Tunisia
8. embroidered head shawl for women

I. Reproduce "Student Activity 25: The Food of Tunisia" for your students. Have them read the information as a large group activity or as an independent reading activity.

Discuss the different types of foods enjoyed by the Tunisian people. Compare the types of foods eaten in Tunisia to the foods eaten in your country. Are there any similarities? Compare cooking styles.

J. Reproduce the "Student Activity 26: The Food of Tunisia" worksheet for your students to be completed independently or in groups. They are to research different Tunisian dishes on the Internet using a search engine such as Google to find out what each one contains. Their findings are to be recorded on the lines provided.

1. a soup with lots of pepper
2. a rich and sticky sorghum and hazelnut cake
3. stew with chickpeas, tomatoes, peppers, garlic, and onions served with a poached egg
4. turnips marinated with lime juice and served with a sauce
5. donuts made with orange juice, deep fried then dipped in honey syrup
6. whole baby lamb baked in a clay case with rosemary
7. sweet peppers stuffed with meat, usually lamb, served with harissa sauce
8. a rich, garlicky soup made with chickpeas

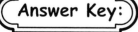
Answer Key:

Tunisia's Culture

K. Reproduce "Student Activity 27: Festivals and Celebrations in Tunisia" for your students. Have them read the information as a large group activity or as an independent reading activity.

Discuss the different celebrations with your students. Have them compare Muslim traditions carried out during celebrations with the traditions pertaining to celebrations in your country. Note the similarities such as giving gifts and treats, visiting family and friends, eating special foods, exchanging cards and gifts, going to a place of worship, celebrating the birthday of a religious prophet.

L. Reproduce the "Student Activity 28: Festivals and Celebrations in Tunisia" worksheet for your students. The students are to record the name of each special day on the line at the end of its description.

1. The Mouled
2. Ramadan
3. Eid al-Idha
4. Islamic New Year
5. Eid al-Fitr
6. Eid-al-Fitr
7. Islamic New Year
8. The Mouled

M. Reproduce "Student Activity 29: Tunisian Music and Dance" for your students. Have your students read the information as a group or as an independent reading activity.

Discuss the types of music and dancing that are done in Tunisia. Point out that many different cultures have left many different traditions in Tunisia.

N. Reproduce the "Student Activity 30: Tunisian Music and Dance" worksheet for your students. This activity can be done in groups or individually. The students are to research Tunisian musical instruments on the Internet using a search engine. A brief description of each one is to be recorded on the lines provided.

Some possible answers are:

1. a stringed instrument with five or six strings
2. two stringed instrument played with a bow
3. a long-necked string instrument with six strings
4. a trapezoid string instrument with 26 strings that is plucked with pieces of horn
5. a stringed musical instrument from India

Going to School in Tunisia

In Tunisia all schools, colleges, and even universities are free for children and adults to attend. We get our books, school supplies, uniforms, and meals free.

The government in Tunisia feels education is very important for its country. It hopes that making schools free to everyone will encourage parents to let their children attend school. In many farming communities people feel it is not important for children to attend school. They feel that they are needed more at home to help care for the animals and work in the fields.

Today, by law, children in Tunisia must go to school between the ages of six to 16. Some children go to preschool at the ages of three to six but their parents must pay a fee. Children from the ages of six to 12 attend a primary school. Some primary schools have different schedules because there are too many students for each class and classrooms have to be shared. One day a class may go to school from 7:30 to 10:00 a.m. and from 1:30 to 3:00 p.m. On another day the class may go to school from 10:00 a.m. to 12:30 p.m.

Lessons in primary school are taught in Arabic and the children learn to read and write in Arabic. The Arabic language is written and read from right to left. The Arabic alphabet has 29 letters plus some small hooks and dashes above or below the letters. Capital letters are written at the ends of words and sentences.

Arabic writing

At the end of the sixth year students must write a special examination. They must pass this exam in order to go to preparatory school. Students from the ages of 12 to 14 attend preparatory schools. The lessons are taught in Arabic or French. After preparatory school, students from the ages of 14 to 18 go to high school. During the first year of high school students take the same subjects. After the first year they take special courses. After high school many students go on to college or university.

Going to School in Tunisia

Even though schools are free in Tunisia, there are still many children who do not go. Our government thinks having an education is very important.

Do you agree with our government?

1. Think of reasons why children in Tunisia need to go to school.

   _____
   _____
   _____
   _____

2. Why do parents in Tunisia keep their children at home?

   _____
   _____

3. Why do children in Tunisia go to school at different times each day?

   _____
   _____

4. How is reading and writing in Arabic different from reading and writing in English?

   _____

5. Tell four things that you learned about the Arabic alphabet.

   _____
   _____
   _____
   _____

6. Tell three things that you learned about going to school in Tunisia.

   _____
   _____
   _____
   _____
   _____

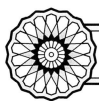

Religion in Tunisia

I am a Muslim and I go to a mosque with my parents every Friday. Our mosque is a big building in the center of a courtyard.

A mosque is a place used for worship and a meeting place, and is a place where scholars study Islam. Most mosques have beautiful domes, minarets, and prayer halls with colorful carpets on the floors. In some countries, a muezzin climbs the minaret to call the faithful to pray five times a day. In Tunisia today, the call to prayer is broadcast on radio and television.

Friday is the Muslim holy day and no one goes to work. The community meets at the mosque to pray. When entering the mosque everyone takes off their shoes and leaves them outside the prayer hall. Upon entering the mosque, a Muslim will use the right foot first while giving blessings to Muhammad and his family. People speak softly in a mosque so not to disturb people who are praying.

The minaret of the old mosque in Tunis

The great mosque in Kairouan, Tunisia

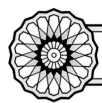
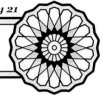

Religion in Tunisia

At the mosque any adult man who knows the prayers can lead the people. Usually a man called an "imam" leads the prayers facing the direction of Mecca. An "imam" is the leader of a mosque. The men stand behind the "imam" and the women stand behind the men. Prayers are recited from the Qur'an and other phrases are said to praise Allah.

The Qur'an, the holy book of Islam

During the prayers the people stand and bow from the waist or kneel with their faces on the floor.

All Muslims believe in the importance of the Five Pillars of Islam which are rules for all Muslims to follow. They are:

- There is only one God and Muhammad was his last prophet. Islam also recognizes Abraham, Moses, and Jesus as prophets.

- A prayer is done five times a day in a special position. The prayers are said at sunrise, midday, afternoon, sunset, and evening. The people must bow and face Mecca. The muezzin calls the people to prayer at the correct times.

A man praying in a mosque

- Muslims are to donate money to help the poor and give money to build and maintain mosques.

- During Ramadan, Muslims are to fast for the entire month during each day from dawn to dusk. Fasting means they must not eat or drink during that time.

- Each Muslim is to travel to Mecca during the 12th month of the lunar calendar once in their lifetime.

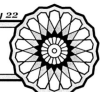

Religion in Tunisia

 Muslims try hard to be kind to people and to lead a good life. They have many rules to follow.

Using a dictionary or the information sheet record a meaning for each of the following words.

1. minaret: _____
_____

2. Islam: _____
_____

3. imam: _____
_____

4. mosque: _____
_____

5. Mecca: _____
_____

6. Qur'an: _____
_____

7. Allah: _____
_____

8. Muhammad: _____
_____

9. prophet: _____
_____

10. muezzin: _____
_____

Tunisian Fashions

Tunisian people dress in many different ways. Some wear modern western fashions while others still dress in traditional ways.

Traditional Berber clothing

is cooler, woollen clothing is worn. Head coverings are worn to protect their heads from the sun.

Traditions in each community affect the style of clothing worn. Married and single women do not dress the same or wear the same head covering. The clothing women wear outside the home is not the same as what is worn inside the home. Clothing used for working on farms is different from clothing worn to the mosque.

Clothing worn in Muslim countries depends on the climate, traditions, religion, and social levels. People who live in a warmer climate usually wear loose clothing to protect themselves from the sun and to keep cool. Their clothes are usually white or light colors because they are cooler. Dark colors such as black attracts the heat. Clothes are made out of cotton. When it

The clothing that Muslims wear is also dictated by the teachings of the Qur'an. Muslim clothing should not attract attention or show off any parts of the body. The only parts that can be shown are the hands and the face. Women are to cover their heads with a "hijab" especially when they enter a mosque. The material used to

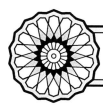

Tunisian Fashions

make clothes must not be so thin that the body can be seen. Clothing should be loose so that the shape of the body can not be seen. Women may not wear wigs or weaves to lengthen their hair nor may they have tattoos on their bodies. Muslims should never wear clothing to look like a non-Muslim. Men wear robes or long shirts that are plain and hang only to their ankles. They must not trail on the ground. Their hair must be neatly cut a little below the ears.

cities. Men dress in business suits and women wear European styles of clothing. Some women wear head coverings while others do not. Sometimes women will wear the traditional light white veil called the "safsari". It is draped over the head, leaving the face free and then it is wrapped around the body to just above the ankles. The safsari is a practical piece of clothing and is popular during winter months and when dusty winds blow in the summer.

Muslim women entering a mosque

A woman in Tunisia

The people in Tunisia dress in a more modern fashion than in other Muslim countries especially in the

Name: _____

Tunisian Fashions

Even though many Tunisians in my country wear modern fashions, the people who live in small villages still wear traditional clothing.

Find out about the traditional clothing worn in Tunisia by using a search engine such as Google on the Internet. Just type in the name of each word below. Find a web site. Write the description on the lines provided.

1. 'arrakiyya: _____
   _____

2. djukha: _____
   _____

3. sebbat: _____
   _____

4. shedda: _____
   _____

5. kabkab: _____
   _____

6. duka: _____
   _____

7. derbala: _____
   _____

8. bakhnuk: _____
   _____

The Food of Tunisia

Tunisians love to eat hot and spicy foods. Our national dish is called "couscous". It is eaten at nearly every one of our meals.

Raw couscous

Couscous is like tiny pasta. It is made from semolina wheat sprinkled with oil and water and rolled into grains. Couscous is cooked in a pot called a couscousiere. Couscous is put in the top of the pot and is cooked by the steam from the meat and vegetables cooking in the bottom of the pot. When everything is cooked the meat, vegetables, and juices are poured over the couscous on a big serving dish.

Tunisians also cook different stews in a pot with a cone-shaped lid called a "tagine". The word "tagine" is also used for the dish cooked in this pot. Tagine makes use of many different kinds of meat, vegetables, and fruits.

Tunisians also like to eat a salad made of tomatoes, onions, peppers, and hardboiled eggs. A soup called "shorba" is made with meat or fish and is usually a meal all by itself. "Kebabs" are made from pieces of lamb, beef, chicken, or fish that are put on long sticks called skewers and broiled or grilled over coals. A spicy, hot sauce called "harissa" made from hot peppers, salt, and garlic is often added to Tunisian dishes.

A popular fast food is "egg brik". It is made of thin pastry with egg, chopped parsley, and capers inside. The pastry is deep fried until the egg is cooked and the pastry is crispy.

For dessert, Tunisians love to eat sweet pastries stuffed with nuts and dates that have been soaked in honey as well as fruits that are in season. They also enjoy drinking strong Turkish coffee and sweet mint tea in glasses.

Since most Tunisians are Muslims, they do not eat pork nor drink alcohol as they are forbidden by their religion.

71

The Food of Tunisia

The dishes that we make and eat come from the many different cultures of people who have lived in our land. Some of our cooking pots are like the ones used by wandering nomads.

Using a search engine such as Google find a web site that describes each of the following Tunisian dishes. Record your information on the lines provided.

1. chorba: _____

   _____

2. bouza: _____

   _____

3. chakchouka: _____

   _____

4. torshi: _____

   _____

5. yo-yo: _____

   _____

6. koucha: _____

   _____

7. felfel mahchi: _____

   _____

8. lalabli: _____

   _____

Festivals and Celebrations in Tunisia

Many of our celebrations have something to do with our religion. We also have festivals that celebrate the different seasons that come during the year.

The first Tunisian celebration is the "Islamic New Year" which falls in the first month of the lunar calendar. When the new moon appears, people go to their mosque to honor Muhammad. The most important part of the day is the telling of the story of Muhammad's escape from Medina to Mecca. Some Muslims exchange New Year's cards and gifts.

In April, the "Mouled" is held. This day celebrates Muhammad's birthday. A special pudding or pastry is made to share with family and friends.

"Ramadan" is a very important Islamic celebration. It does not always fall at the same time each year. During the 30 days of Ramadan, Muslims fast from dawn to dusk and only work for six hours a day. During fasting, Muslims do not eat, drink, smoke, or even chew gum. When dusk comes the people eat their favorite foods and visit family and friends. During Ramadan, money is given to the poor and the mosques.

Ramadan ends with the festival of "Eid al-Fitr", the Feast of the Breaking of the Fast, which lasts three days. Muslims wear their finest clothes and hang lights and other decorations in their homes. Gifts are given to children and families meet and feast with friends.

Another important celebration for Muslims is the "Eid al-Idha", the Feast of Sacrifice. It lasts for three days and celebrates the story of Ibraham, from the Qur'an. Ibraham was about to kill his son as a sacrifice to Allah when a voice spoke to him and stopped him. A ram appeared and Ibraham was told to use it instead as an offering to Allah. To honor Ibraham's trust in Allah, Muslims sacrifice sheep, goats, and camels and give the meat to the poor.

Tunisians love life and enjoy celebrating it with festivals. Every small village or town holds festivals. These festivals are held to celebrate the summer, the harvest, the fishing season, a local saint, or the coming of spring. At these festivals people dance traditional dances, sing folk songs, eat special foods, and watch camels race in the desert.

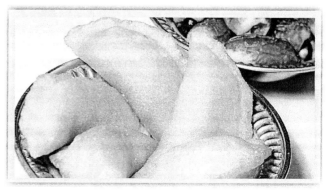

A meal to break the fast of Ramadan

OTM -123 • SSA1-23 All About Tunisia

Festivals and Celebrations in Tunisia

Celebrations are very important to the people in Tunisia. Eid al-Fitr is my favorite. During this celebration I get treats and new clothes.

How much do you remember about celebrations in Tunisia?

Match the name of the celebration to the sentence that describes it.

Islamic New Year   **Eid al-Fitr**   **Eid al-Idha**
The Mouled   **Ramadan**

1. People in Tunisia celebrate the birthday of a great Muslim.

   _____

2. Muslims must not eat or drink from dawn to dusk each day for a whole month.

   _____

3. Ibraham's bravery and faith are honored.

   _____

4. Tunisians watch the sky in order to see the new moon.

   _____

5. Homes are decorated with lights and everyone in the family wears their best clothes.

   _____

6. A month's fast is broken with this three-day feast.

   _____

7. Muslim children enjoy hearing the story about Muhammad and his great escape from Medina to Mecca.

   _____

8. A special pudding or pastry is made as a special treat to celebrate this important day.

   _____

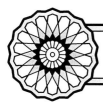

Tunisian Music and Dance

Many of our songs and dances are traditional ones. Some come from a mixture of different cultures while many are Arabic.

Traditional music played on the street at tea time

Music is important to the people in Tunisia. Many of the people living in small towns and villages still love to sing and dance the ancient songs of the desert, love, their country, beauty, and nature. Poetry and music are used together and many Arabic poems are sung as songs. Folk music was sung around campfires, in homes, and as a part of celebrations such as weddings. Entertainers often traveled from place to place to entertain in towns and cities. Entertainers are still seen on the city streets today in Tunisia.

Arabic music is played and listened to in Tunisia. It does not have any harmony which means the sounds do not blend together. The music is sung or played in a solo or by a single musician. Sometimes groups of musicians repeat what has been sung or played without any harmony.

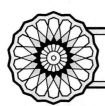

Tunisian Music and Dance

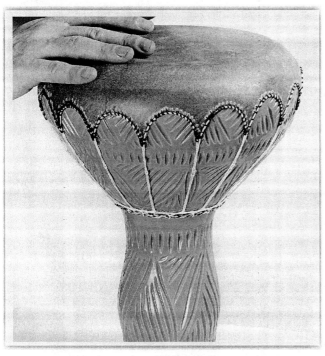

A darbuka is a traditional Arabic drum

Arabic traditional music is not written but is passed down in an apprentice system where the teacher shows the student. Musicians learn to play music "by ear" and by listening to others.

"Malouf" is a kind of Spanish music that is played and listened to in Tunisia as well. It is performed with musical instruments such as violins, drums, lutes, and sitars. A sitar is an Indian musical instrument. Malouf is very rhythmic music that is often performed at weddings and other special ceremonies.

A lute

Dancing in a Muslim country is viewed differently than in other countries. Some Muslims feel dance should not be done at all. They feel dancing is sinful. Other Muslims feel folk dancing just between men and just between women is fine. Men and women are not to dance with each other.

Many folk dances are done with separate groups of men and women but not mixed. These dances celebrate famous warriors, the planting seasons, the harvest, and the changes in the seasons. Some dances celebrate special times in a person's life such as weddings and births.

Tunisian Music and Dance

In Tunisia our music is played on traditional instruments. Some of these instruments come from other countries as many different people have lived in our country.

Using a search engine such as Google, research on the Internet to find out information about each of the following instruments. Record your information on the lines provided.

1. oud: _____
_____
_____
_____

2. Persian fiddle: _____
_____
_____
_____

3. sax: _____
_____
_____
_____

4. qanun: _____
_____
_____
_____

5. sitar: _____
_____
_____
_____

Tunisia's History

A. Reproduce "Student Activity 31: Tunisia' History" for your students. Using a search engine on the Internet such as Google have your students research one of the civilizations that have controlled Tunisia in the past. The information is to be recorded on the lines provided. This activity could be completed in small groups or independently.

On the chalkboard list the names of the various civilizations that have controlled Tunisia in chronological order as you discuss each one with your class.

1. Phoenicians   2. Romans   3. Vandals   4. Byzantine Empire
5. Arabs   6. Turkey   7. France

Tunisia's History:

Modern Tunis, the capital city of Tunisia, was once the ancient city of Carthage. It was first ruled by the Phoenicians. The Phoenicians were considered one of the greatest peoples of the ancient world. They were great sailors, navigators, and traders who lived along the coastline of the Mediterranean Sea. Carthage was destroyed in 146 B.C. because of the rivalry between the Romans and the Phoenicians.

The Romans ruled in this area for several centuries. In about the fourth century after Christ, the Romans were driven out by the Vandals. The Vandals were a tribe of barbarians that invaded the West Roman Empire with the help of other barbarians and destroyed the Roman Empire in this area. Between 300 A.D. and 500 A.D., the Vandals controlled the Mediterranean Sea and countries along its coast. During the sixth century after Christ, it became part of the Byzantine Empire which was a part of the Roman Empire known as the East Roman Empire.

In the seventh century, Carthage was captured by the Arabs and was once again destroyed. It is these ruins that form a part of modern Tunis.

During the sixteenth century, Turkey gained control of Tunisia. A Turkish governor lead the government. During this period of Turkish rule, Tunisia became a haven for many pirate ships. They used Tunisia's coastline as a home and base for their pirate ships. These pirate ships often robbed and killed crews and travelers on ships that belonged to France and Italy. They would steal whatever the ships carried. Both countries wanted to control Tunisia and became rivals for its control. France wanted to extend its Algerian borders to include Tunisia. Italy wanted control because a large number of Italians already lived there. In 1881, French troops took over Tunisia and the country became a French protectorate in 1883. The French ruled Tunisia until 1956.

After World War II, Tunisia began to demand its independence. In 1955, Tunisians gained partial self-government and in 1956, France agreed to its complete independence.

B. Reproduce "Student Activity 32: Tunisia's Cities" for your students. Have them work in groups or independently to complete the research activity.

Tunisia's History

Tunisia has a very interesting history. Many different people have invaded our country in the past.

Choose one of the names from the following list. Using a search engine on the Internet or encyclopedias in the library, research the civilization or country that you chose. Record the facts that you find on the lines provided.

Phoenicians   Vandals   France   Byzantine Empire   Arabs   Romans   Turkey

_____

_____

_____

_____

_____

_____

_____

_____

_____

_____

_____

_____

_____

_____

_____

_____

Name: _____

Tunisia's Cities

We have many old and interesting cities in Tunisia. Tourists come from all over the world to visit them.

Choose one of the places from the list below. Find out its location in Tunisia, its size, its population, and the interesting sights found in it. Use the Internet, encyclopedias, and other reference books to help you. Record these facts on the lines provided.

Places in Tunisia

Tunis, Sfax, Sousse, Bizerte, Kairouan, Jerba, Matmâta, Gabes

_____

_____

_____

_____

_____

_____

_____

_____

_____

_____

_____

_____

_____